LIFE IS CHAOS
AND ALL IS WELL

HOW TO LIVE YOUR BEST LIFE IN TODAY'S
UNCERTAIN WORLD

WINNING CHAOS

Paperback ISBN: 979-8-9912541-0-6
Ebook ISBN: 979-8-9912541-1-3
Audiobook ISBN: 979-8-9912541-2-0

First edition September 2024

winningchaos.com

For Jacquii, the love of my life and best friend. Thank you for the long walks and talks, for keeping me afloat when I had nothing left, for your love and encouragement, for holding the mirror up, and for accompanying me on this wonderful journey.

For Katie and Riley. Being your father has taught me more about living than I'd ever imagined. Most of all, it has taught me the kind of person I want to be.

PREFACE

What is happening in the world today? Many days, I wake up and think, what a mess! There's so much anger, fear, and hurt. There are power struggles on every level of society. Some win and take all, while others lose. The notion that what's good for the community is good for me has been replaced with what's good for me is good for me, and all others be dammed!

It's a time of change like we have never experienced before. Families are changing. Children are growing up facing challenges many of us never knew. Our environment is changing, and our planet is warming, with consequences for all living things, including us.

We seem ill equipped to deal with the ensuing chaos. We're less tolerant, quicker to anger, more self-righteous, and, at times, just mean. The more we experience change and chaos, the more we feel chaotic and less in control.

Several years ago, my older brother and I launched a consulting firm in Asheville, NC. The company provided leadership development, business planning, and strategic thinking workshops for leaders and managers in business, manufacturing, government, and non-profits.

At the time, I was finishing up a master's degree in human resources and organizational development. On Friday afternoons, we often workshopped ideas and theories around leadership, integrity, and values. These are some of my best memories of that time. I was energized, learning, and engaged! We were both "in the zone." In one of those sessions, David shared something he'd begun writing called *Life Is Chaos, and All Is Well*. We worked on it and came up with a one-page overview of the chaos of life. Over the years, I've reworked sections, edited, and added to it. For me, it's been a mantra and become a core philosophy I try to live by. Here it is in its current form.

LIFE IS CHAOS, AND ALL IS WELL

Stop wishing for an illusion. There is no other reality than the one in front of us. Bad things happen to good people. Children die of cancer, and people get abused and battered. Systems are not perfect and never will be. Good intentions do not always pay off. Commitment does not always deliver. Treating others as you would have them treat you does not always work. Life is chaos.

If we're honest with ourselves, we are very self-centered, and why should we be any different? After all, aren't survival and self-preservation paramount to all else? This can disappoint, sadden, and depress us. We can become angry, bitter, and hateful. Or we can realize that this is the way things are. Life is chaos.

Yet, in chaos there is hope. There is power and opportunity for each of us to reach our potential. When we begin letting go of our illusions about life, things, and other people and stop reacting in dismay, frustration, anger, and hurt, we will start to experience the seeds of our own liberation. When we begin living life as it is, rather than as we wish it to be, we will start experiencing freedom. All is well.

This is one of the great paradoxes of life. There can be real chaos in our lives and, at the same time, the potential for great growth and healing. When we begin to wake up and become aware that our lives can be unchained from the slavery of our illusions, we can truly start to live in the world as fulfilled, happy people, and in the process, play our part in its transformation. Life is chaos, and all is well.

TABLE OF CONTENTS

INTRODUCTION

AS I BEGAN WRITING THIS book, I started thinking of the stories my father told my brothers and me when we were children. They came from recollections of his childhood growing up in the 1930s in Eastern Kentucky. My father called them the Dewberry Creek Stories, the adventures of two kids and the challenges they faced growing up poor but with a strong sense of family and community. These tales provided my brothers and me with a connection to our past. They reinforced my parents' values and how people are expected to act and behave. These stories, like those humans have been telling each other for millennia, are important and help us make meaning of things. As humans, we love a good story that explains who we are, where we came from, and why things happen. Over thousands of years, we have created stories, religions, philosophies, constructs, archetypes, and theories to try to answer these fundamental questions.

Ultimately, this is why I've written this book. I'm not a psychologist, counselor, or therapist. As someone just trying to make it through each day, I recognize the chaos in my own life. I've been in pain and felt loss. I've also experienced true joy and fulfillment. Through examining my life and experiencing it with others, I've realized that even though there is chaos, all is well.

I'm not sure you would describe this as a self-help book. However, I've attempted to share ideas and insights that you may find helpful. I've shared stories from my own life as a father, husband, son, brother, friend, recovering tech entrepreneur, change agent, and someone who strives—but doesn't always succeed—at living his best life every day. While writing this book, I've talked with friends and colleagues much wiser than me. They have listened patiently and provided me with valuable knowledge and insights.

I've divided this book into two parts. Part one concerns living in chaos—in our families, workplaces, and interactions. Here, I explore chaos' external and internal impact on our wellbeing, relationships, and overall lives.

Part two is about living a fulfilling life despite the chaos, embracing the idea that *all is well*. This section offers actionable insights into living our best lives, transitioning from chaos to a place of abundance. I also do a deep dive into concepts like awareness, choices, and authenticity.

Throughout the book, there are real-life case studies and anecdotes from my own experiences, as well as those of friends, family, and acquaintances. While the stories are authentic, some names and details have been altered for privacy and confidentiality.

Each chapter wraps up with practical life hacks—valuable tips and tricks gleaned from personal and shared experiences to navigate life more effectively. I've divided the life hacks into three categories: mindfulness, journaling, and action. Whether amid chaos or living in the *all is well*, I've found these practices useful in my own life.

MINDFULNESS hacks include practices like meditation and breathwork. Practicing mindfulness allows us to have a deeper understanding of our thoughts, emotions, and experiences. It's about observing and reflecting on an emotion or event without trying to fix or change it. We become aware of them, realize that they don't define us, accept that they're there, then move on. Numerous apps and resources online teach mindfulness and meditation, which can be useful for developing and guiding your own practice.

JOURNALING hacks are based on proven techniques that allow us to organize our thoughts and feelings while gaining new insight into them as we prepare to set goals and take action. If you're new to journaling, I suggest you establish a time and place to do your journaling regularly—it could be when you first wake up to set your intentions for the day or before you go to sleep to reflect on your day. Choose a quiet place where you won't be disturbed and write in the same place daily. In my experience, even five minutes of journaling each day is beneficial. The goal is to establish a routine and stick with it.

ACTION hacks are suggested ways for putting your mindfulness and journalling "work" into practice. Before deciding on your action steps, I recommend that you ask yourself these questions:

- ❖ Will my action detract from or add value to the situation or others?

- ❖ What outcome(s) do I want to achieve?

- ❖ Have I carefully planned my action?

- ❖ Are there potential negative consequences or risks for myself or others? If so, how can I mitigate them?

PART ONE

LIFE IS CHAOS

1
WHAT IS CHAOS?

CHAOS REFERS TO A STATE OF disorder and confusion in which events, actions, and people are unpredictable. A lack of control and order characterizes it. Chaos can occur in different parts of our lives, including personal, social, and environmental.

Imagine waking up one morning all set to rock your day only to have chaos crash the party. Your carefully laid plans fall apart as unexpected events and situations unfold. You're left confused, uncertain, and often spiraling out of control. Sometimes, it can feel like you're walking on a tightrope with no safety net, where fear, anxiety, and a rollercoaster of other emotions characterize your every step.

Many of us experience constant chaos. It's like a storm has descended upon us, and we can't escape it. Then, the resulting stress, pain, frustration, anger, and trauma can be overwhelming and even crippling. Life is chaos!

Think about the times in your life when you've experienced chaos. Many days, I've wanted to stay in bed and not face the world due to the turmoil around me. One thing I've found helpful in keeping me going amid chaos is to name and understand what I am dealing with. Once I know the chaos I'm experiencing, I can develop strategies to cope and flourish.

Here's a personal example. When I was 12, on a torrid summer day in Charlotte, NC, I was playing with friends in a park. We were having a water fight on a jungle gym when I slipped and fell. I was rushed to the hospital in a lot of pain and with internal bleeding. After a night in the hospital, the doctors figured out what was happening, rushed me into surgery, and removed my spleen.

I spent eight days in the ICU. I came close to dying but only realized that by the worried look on my parents' faces. I spent the rest of the summer at home recuperating while my brothers and friends enjoyed their vacation time playing outside. I felt disconnected from my family and friends for the first time during that bizarre summer, and it was scary.

To make matters worse, my brothers went off to camp, and my parents went somewhere too—I like to think they were working and not sitting on a beach somewhere. I felt alone. Fortunately, my aunt Jeanette showed up to take care of me. She was a great aunt—kind, smart, inquisitive, and honest.

Toward the end of summer, I began feeling nervous about returning to school. What would my friends think of me? I wasn't the same person they knew the previous year. I'd had a near-death experience and now had a huge, ugly purple scar on my belly that made me feel self-conscious. I refused to take my shirt off in front of others.

Aunt Jeanette, sensing my stress and anxiety, asked me what was going on. I told her, and she said in her strong Eastern Kentucky accent, "Well, honey, you are different! You'll never be the same as you were before. Now, you can sit there and feel what you're feeling, or you can realize that you've been through the fire and water, and you're a new, changed, and different person."

Aunt Jeanette helped me understand and name the chaos I was experiencing. She challenged me to accept it and see the opportunities going forward. For this, I'm forever grateful.

Chaos has occurred in all our lives and will continue to do so. Our challenge is to recognize it for what it is and develop support strategies and a mindset that helps us navigate the chaos and keep going.

Internal and External Chaos

At the time of writing this book, the world is in a state of chaos. There is war, disease, pandemics, poverty, homelessness, and environmental destruction. I'm amazed at how chaotic our lives have become over the past few years. We spend less time working on real interpersonal relationships and more time fostering virtual ones. Our political landscape has become a world in which absolutism has replaced negotiation and compromise, one where the needs and wants of the few outweigh those of the many.

I've identified three main types of chaos: internal, external, and environmental. I'll only explore the realms of internal and external chaos here, leaving the discussion of environmental chaos for another time.

Internal and External Chaos

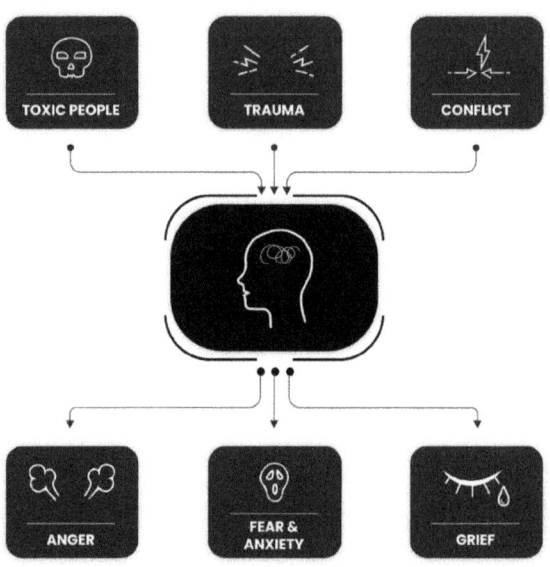

Internal chaos originates within ourselves—our emotions, decisions, actions, thoughts, and beliefs. This type of chaos is deeply intertwined with our self-awareness and how we perceive ourselves, our surroundings, and others. Our mental, physical, and emotional wellbeing greatly influence the levels of chaos we experience. Internal chaos can encompass feelings of depression, fear, anxiety, and grief, among other emotions. As someone who suffers from anxiety, I've noticed that when I'm anxious, things feel more chaotic.

External chaos, on the other hand, encompasses the disruptive forces from outside sources, such as events and people. These can throw our lives into disarray or create an atmosphere where chaos thrives. Think of the traumas, toxic people, and conflicts that challenge us in our personal and professional lives.

Often, we experience more than one form of chaos at a time. Sometimes, we experience the trifecta with internal, external, and environmental all at once. This is because chaos feeds off chaos. Our external chaos can influence our internal chaos, leading to increased chaos in our interpersonal relationships, personal wellbeing, and workplace relationships and performance.

Amid the chaos, routines are shattered, and obstacles appear, disappear, and reappear out of thin air. It's as if life hits the reset button, throwing us off balance. However, this chaos and reset cycle can have a silver lining. Chaos forces us to tap into our creativity, making us think on our feet and find innovative solutions to navigate it. Suddenly, we can break free from the chaos to discover other opportunities and our hidden potential. As we enter this state, we are moving from the Life Is Chaos into the All Is Well.

2
INTERNAL CHAOS

INTERNAL CHAOS IS CHAOS THAT influences normal emotions and responses in ways that can harm our self-worth, relationships, and work. It is often triggered by trauma, conflict, and toxic people. One of the challenges I've faced in my own life is how to manage my anger, fear, or anxiety and still show up every day ready to work and live. Here, I've chosen to focus on fear and anxiety, grief and anger, as they're the essence of internal chaos and, when not dealt with effectively, can have a major impact on all aspects of our lives.

3

FEAR AND ANXIETY

I'M A SCI-FI NERD, DRAWN TO the genre because of its rich storytelling. One of my favorite characters from the Star Wars universe is Yoda, a wise Jedi Master, a mentor, and a philosopher. One of Yoda's teachings that resonates with me is about fear. In a conversation with young Anakin Skywalker, another central figure of the series, Yoda senses Anakin's fear. Anakin brushes it off, questioning its significance. However, Yoda emphasizes its importance, stating that fear only leads to negative states of being and emotions.

Is fear really that significant? After all, we've all faced fear in our lives. For children, fear serves as a guide, helping them navigate danger and stay safe. Still, for those of us who struggle with fear and anxiety, it's a different story.

Fear and anxiety are often discussed together because they're closely intertwined, often emerging as unwelcome companions amid life's chaos. Sometimes, I find myself sighing heavily throughout the day. Usually, it's not because I'm feeling overwhelmed by life itself but by my own fears and anxiety about it.

When I was 19, I took a year off from college and traveled, worked, and went on an Outward Bound course. I remember asking one of my rock-climbing instructors if he was still afraid when he climbed. He explained that although he had confidence in his abilities and the equipment, he also had a little fear, which was good. It kept him focused and on his toes. He said if he ever stopped feeling afraid, he'd stop climbing because he believed without it, he could become reckless and unsafe. So, some fear can be useful. It can protect us. However, too much fear in our lives is not so helpful.

The challenge with fear lies in its normalization amid chaos. Corporations often exploit fear through tactics like FOMO (fear of missing out) to boost sales. Similarly, fear is wielded by religions, governments, politicians, and people in power to motivate and control others.

Fear also helps us when we're faced with perceived danger. Our bodies rely on this primal survival mechanism deeply ingrained in our evolutionary past. The fight, flight, or freeze response kicks in automatically when confronted with a threat, like encountering a bear in the woods. While these responses are instinctual and geared toward survival, they come with inherent risks and don't always yield optimal outcomes.

As adults, living in a perpetual state of fear or anxiety can have a major impact on our physical, mental, and emotional wellbeing. Constant exposure to fear triggers our body's stress response, causing a rush of adrenaline and cortisol to prepare us for action. While these hormones serve a purpose, continued high levels can be detrimental. It's like our body is overdosing on its own chemicals, potentially leading to cellular damage and increasing the risk of conditions like heart disease, cancer, and diabetes. Additionally, chronic fear and stress can affect our brain, emotions, libido, and interpersonal relationships.

While fear and anxiety are genuine emotions typically triggered by real danger or distressing circumstances, they can stem from many sources, such as relationships, financial concerns, and familial responsibilities.

One of the wild things about fear and anxiety is that when we're experiencing them, they can sometimes intensify each other—as shown in this diagram. This can lead to a cycle in which fear and anxiety feed off one another, even when there's no real danger present. It's a great example of internal chaos.

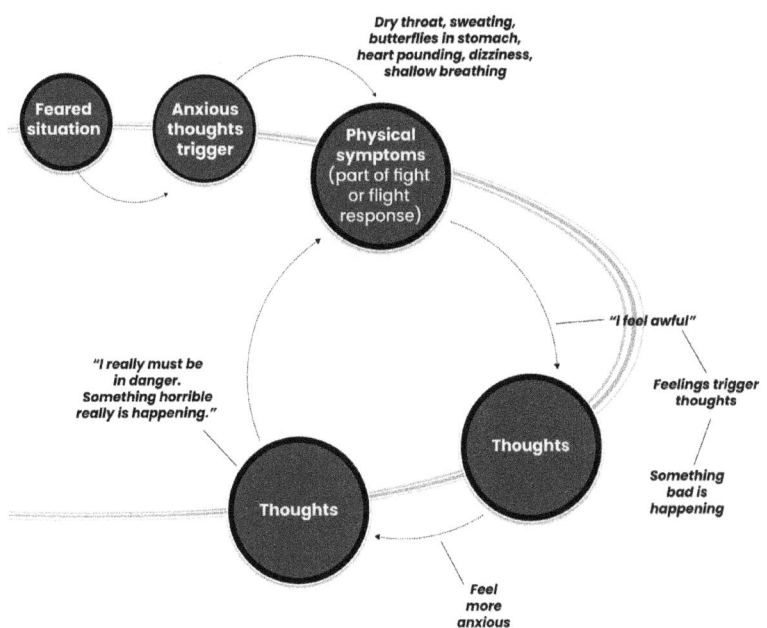

The Cycle of Anxiety

SOURCE: MINDWELL LEEDS

A lifetime of fear and anxiety

Throughout my life, fear and anxiety have been constant companions. As a child, I struggled with various fears, from being left alone to not being included in a group or team, and even the fear of death. These fears and anxieties came and went. However, one fear that has persisted into adulthood is the fear of being perceived as incompetent or unworthy. I worry that people will look at me and realize the emperor has no clothes! I often find myself consumed with anxiety, sometimes over events that have not even occurred.

I spend a lot of time and energy guessing about the underlying meanings of emails and phone calls, often fearing they contain negative judgments about me. When I don't hear back from people whom I've called or emailed, or things don't happen when I think they should, I create fictional scenarios that only intensify my anxiety. Basically, I write my own fiction. Each time, I feel my heart racing, caught in a cycle that I know isn't healthy and negatively affects those around me.

My wife once questioned whether I might have Generalized Anxiety Disorder (GAD), characterized by excessive worrying, even in the absence of clear reasons. While I initially dismissed the notion, I acknowledge that my fears and anxieties often spiral out of control, leaving me feeling overwhelmed. However, through self-awareness and seeking help, I've come to realize the impact my fear and anxiety has on myself and my loved ones.

As I've grown older, I've made a concerted effort to address my anxiety more intentionally. My wife has been a huge help, offering perspective and reminding me to consider the worst-case scenario, which often reveals I can handle whatever comes my way. Meditation, self-awareness, and breathing exercises have really helped me manage these emotions. While they may always be there, I've learned that with hard work and resilience, I can prevent them from controlling my life.

Story: Shootout In Iriba

In 2013, I had the privilege of launching and working with an international non-profit focused on tackling energy poverty in Africa. As part of this effort, we collaborated with innovative solar companies worldwide. Our first partnership was with the United Nations High Commission for Refugees (UNHCR). We were tasked with conducting a field study and authoring a report on the lighting and energy needs of refugees in camps in Sub-Saharan Africa, which involved traveling to Africa and spending time in refugee camps.

Our initial project was in Chad, specifically in four refugee camps in Eastern Chad on the border with Sudan. These camps housed approximately 400,000 refugees who had fled Sudan during the Darfur crisis. After arriving in N'djamena, the capital of Chad, a colleague and I headed straight to the UN offices.

After getting our security badges, we went to our first security briefing, which was conducted in French. Growing up in Western North Carolina and having spent much of my life in Australia, I had never learned French, nor had my colleague. We asked the security officer if he spoke any English, to which he simply replied, "No," and continued his briefing in French.

After a few minutes, I found the humor in the whole situation. The security officer was obviously giving us crucial information, but we had no idea what he was saying. It reminded me of long-ago

Sundays in church as a kid when my brothers and I would giggle at something the minister said. My colleague also found it amusing and we began to laugh out loud. The security guard looked at us sternly but continued the briefing. After it concluded, we found an English-speaking staff member who summarized the briefing for us:

- ❖ We would be flying to a town called Iriba in Eastern Chad near the border with Sudan.

- ❖ We were to stay in the UN compound at all times, which was a walled compound with armed guards.

- ❖ Each day, we would load into a white Toyota Land Cruiser and meet in the center of town. Other aid agencies would join us in their Land Cruisers, and we would travel in a convoy to a refugee camp.

- ❖ Chadian Army troops would protect the convoy in Toyota pickup trucks at the front and back of the convoy. They were complete badasses—mirrored sunglasses, AK-47s, no smiles, all business.

- ❖ We were never to go to the camps without an armed escort.

- ❖ The area was dangerous, with armed groups roaming around. These groups regularly held up unescorted vehicles and robbed the passengers. If we were ever held up, we should give them whatever they asked for and not fight or run. These groups were also known for kidnapping aid workers and holding them hostage for ransom. There had not been a kidnapping in the past six months, so she thought we would be fine.

When I heard about the security situation, I feared going to such a place. I also felt like an idiot for laughing during the all-French security briefing.

The next day, we arrived at the airport in N'djamena and boarded the 16-seat propeller plane with a big blue UN on the side. Our pilot was a large South African woman who reminded me of Agatha Trunchbull from Roald Dahl's *Matilda*—no-nonsense and slightly scary. Once we boarded, she gave her safety speech and radioed the tower, then we taxied down the runway and took off to Iriba.

Iriba is a small town where multiple relief agencies housed their aid workers within walled compounds. There were three nearby refugee camps—Iridimi, Touloum, and Am Nabak—housing about 50,000 refugees.

Visiting the camps was a great experience. We met some incredible people and began our survey of lighting and energy needs, installing several different types of lights to test.

On the last day, we were supposed to head out to one of the camps at 8:00 AM, but at 6:30 AM, the head of the UN compound, Felix, pounded on my bedroom door. "Get up! Get up! Pack quickly. You're being evacuated. Be ready in 15 minutes!" I had no idea what was happening, but I knew it was serious. I quickly packed and met my colleague out front. We were loaded into a Land Cruiser. This time, we had one Chadian soldier driving and one in the front passenger seat.

We arrived at Iriba's airport, where 80 people were already gathered. These were staff members from the other aid agencies who were also being evacuated. Felix explained that early that morning, staff from another aid agency decided to make a quick trip to one of the camps unescorted. Their driver was new, and bandits held them up. The driver tried to make a run for it, and the bandits opened fire, riddling the Land Cruiser with bullets. The driver was killed, and three aid workers were seriously injured.

Then, we heard machine gun fire from the bushes near the airstrip. Chaos ensued. People were yelling, soldiers were firing into the bushes, and we huddled behind a small building that acted as a radio tower and airport office.

As this was happening, the UN plane landed. Aid workers gathered around, pushing for a place in line to grab one of the 16 seats. Total chaos! I didn't like my chances of getting on the flight, but Felix assured me we would be on it. With a few Chadian soldiers at his back, Felix calmed the crowd and pointed to 10 people, including my colleague and I, who would fly on the first flight out. We waited as the South African Trunchbull exited the plane and began barking orders. Six seats were removed to make room for the injured.

Two pickup trucks pulled up alongside the plane, carrying the injured aid workers—one in a wheelchair, two on stretchers. Trunchbull got in the cockpit and yelled, "Right, you people, fasten your seat belts." There was no safety check. She pushed the throttle, and we took off. As we ascended, I looked down to see an aid worker on the stretcher next to me, covered in blood and bandages with an IV. I was afraid and thought, *What the fuck are you doing here, Huff?*

Reflecting on this event, I still remember the incredibly intense fear and anxiety I felt. It took me some time, talking with people and journaling, to deal with the fear and anxiety of this experience. However, it was nothing compared to what the remaining aid workers must have felt. Fortunately, things calmed down after a few months, and I was able to make a couple more trips to Iriba to continue our work. I visited several other camps in Africa during this time, but this was by far the most memorable experience. A year later, I tabled a report on lighting needs in refugee camps in Sub-Saharan Africa to the Shelter Committee of the UNHCR in Geneva. The report was dedicated to the four aid workers involved in the shootout.

The wild thing about fear and anxiety is that we don't need to be involved in a shootout to experience it. It can be present throughout our lives. The challenge is in developing strategies for coping, letting it go, and moving on.

LIFE HACKS

Below are a few of the things that help me deal with feelings of anxiety and fear. Give them a try to see if they work for you too.

MINDFULNESS

BREATHE: Remember, when you're experiencing feelings of fear and anxiety, your body is in stress response mode, so the first thing you need to do is calm that response. There's a lot of new research on the benefits of breathing and how it can reduce feelings of anxiety. A couple of the methods I like are box breathing and 4-7-8 breathing. You can check out these and other methods online. My favorite is to take two to three short inhales through the nose and then slowly exhale through the mouth. While doing this, I think about the things I'm grateful for. By shifting to gratitude, my fear and anxiety soon melt away.

Journaling

WORST-CASE SCENARIO: A great journaling activity is to ask what the worst that can happen is. Be honest and keep your answers relevant to the situation at hand. It may not be nice, but at least you've identified it. You may also find that it's not as bad as you imagined.

Actions

DISTRACT YOURSELF: Get up and move—walk around the block, put on some music and dance, make yourself a coffee, take a hot bath, create some art, call a friend. Whatever it is, a distraction will give your mind a chance to settle and your body time to unwind.

4

GRIEF

WE ALL GO THROUGH PERIODS OF sadness, grief, and pain. However, in our society there are unspoken rules about how we should deal with grief.

❖ Rule 1: Buck up and deal with it silently. Don't complain.

❖ Rule 2: Someone always has it worse, so your grief isn't valid.

I call bullshit on these societal norms. We must acknowledge and express our grief, regardless of our background or circumstance. Grief, pain, and sadness are universal experiences, and it's healthy to confront them openly.

In college, I took a psychology course as an elective. I remember learning about the grief cycle developed by Elisabeth Kübler-Ross. Through studying the emotional and psychological responses to loss, she identified five stages of grief: denial, anger, bargaining, depression, and acceptance. The stages of grief aren't a strict road-map; instead, they acknowledge the complex and individual nature of the grieving process. Grief is not a cyclical process. We enter it at different stages and move around it as we try to understand and make meaning of the loss. It's also important to note that not everyone will experience all these stages, and the order and duration of each stage can vary greatly.

❖ DENIAL: This initial stage serves as a defense mechanism against the shock and overwhelming emotions of loss. People may refuse to accept the reality, clinging to the hope that it's all a mistake or a bad dream. Denial provides a temporary shield, allowing us to process the news gradually. It's like a buffer zone, giving the mind time to adjust to the harsh reality. I've seen people who "check out" when faced with overwhelming emotions. While denial helps protect us, it's important not to stay checked out.

❖ ANGER: As the reality of the loss sinks in, the pain of the loss becomes more apparent, often leading to frustration, resentment, and anger. This anger can be directed outward toward others, the universe, or even inward toward ourself. It's a natural response to the perceived injustice of the situation as we struggle with the unfairness of our loss. This stage is characterized by powerlessness and a desire to find someone or something to blame. I know someone who has been stuck in the anger stage for most of her life. She's now 83, and every time she loses someone, experiences trauma, or has a major change in her life, her grief goes right back to anger. The sad thing is she doesn't see it or how it affects those around her.

❖ BARGAINING: In this stage, we try to regain control by making deals or seeking alternatives. We might engage in "if only" or "what if" statements, fantasizing about ways to undo or prevent the loss. This stage often involves reaching out to a higher power or seeking meaning amid chaos. It's a desperate attempt to negotiate with fate, hoping for a different outcome.

❖ DEPRESSION: As the full weight of the loss sinks in, we may experience profound sadness, emptiness, and despair. This stage is characterized by withdrawal, loss of interest in daily activities, and a sense of hopelessness about the future. It's a period of mourning in which we confront the reality of our loss and struggle with the void it leaves behind. Depression during grief is different from clinical depression, but they share similarities. It's important to seek support if needed during this vulnerable time.

❖ ACCEPTANCE: The final stage of the grief model involves coming to terms with the reality of the loss and integrating it into our lives. Acceptance doesn't mean that the pain disappears or that everything is okay. Rather, it signifies a gradual acknowledgment of the new reality and a willingness to move forward. I know from experience that acceptance is a process; it's difficult, and it can take time to reach this stage fully. I also know that life is chaos, and I can find myself back in grief at any time. My hope is that each time I go back into it, I'll have a little more understanding, and perhaps, it'll hurt less.

Grief is deeply personal, and the stages have no set timeline or order. Some move through it quickly, while others linger. The model is a guide, not a rulebook, helping us navigate loss and trauma.

During the writing of this book, my father died. He was an amazing man, and I miss him. He died slowly of congestive heart failure. In the last two years of his life, we thought we were losing him many times, so the grief has been long and drawn out. While I've been dealing with my own grief and sense of loss, I've also observed how my family, particularly my brothers, have been grieving. We're all different people, so it stands to reason that we're each dealing with our dad's passing in different ways.

As he was dying, the three of us drew closer together. We had many conversations about our childhood, our father, and how we were dealing with the dying process. We were fortunate that we all got to say goodbye and tell him how much we loved him. And yet, we all seemed to be left wanting more—more time, more conversations, more honesty, and more closure.

Maybe that's the hard part about grief. Even though Dad is gone, we still have unresolved expectations. All I can do is cherish the memories, let go of the pain, and move forward. However, knowing that doesn't make me feel less sadness.

Today, our lives are filled with chaos and change, exacerbating feelings of grief. From environmental crises to societal upheaval, loss surrounds us. Life is chaos. Yet, amidst this chaos, we must acknowledge our grief and support one another.

Story: Losing A Child

One of my deepest fears in life is the thought of losing one of my children. When they were younger, my role was to protect, guide, nurture, and keep them safe. Now that they're young adults, our relationship has evolved, but the fear still lingers. My heart goes out to anyone who has experienced the loss of a child.

I have friends who tragically lost their young adult son a few years ago. He was a great guy, full of life, funny, and lit up a room wherever he went. The circumstances surrounding his death remain uncertain, adding to the immense pain his parents endure. Questions about what happened and why haunt them even after five years. I've watched this couple wrestle with their grief in very different ways; sometimes, they're in the same grief stage together, and other times, they're in different stages. They've sought solace in faith, only to lose it, and tried finding meaning in their daily lives, but they're changed people.

The father has thrown himself into work, struggling with anger and disappointment. Legal action provided some compensation, but it didn't ease his anguish or fill the hole in his heart. The mother has played out her grief on social media, often alienating friends and colleagues and lashing out at people online. Her pain is raw and palpable, manifesting in anger and sorrow.

Though they're slowly rebuilding their lives, the pain of their loss remains ever-present. Triggers, like certain words or sights, can plunge them right back into the depths of grief. My heart aches for them, but I remain hopeful that they'll eventually find peace.

Navigating chaos and grief

Grief following the loss of a loved one is expected, but as I mentioned earlier, we can also experience grief during chaos. Finding your way out can feel daunting when surrounded by chaos. Denial, anger, bargaining, and depression all come calling—sometimes in unison, other times repeatedly—clouding your perspective. It's typically only when you reach the stage of acceptance that you can move on.

One of my favorite scenes from *Forrest Gump* illustrates this journey. Lieutenant Dan comes to work with Forest on the shrimp boat. He's bitter and angry. Life hasn't turned out like he'd hoped. He's lost both his legs and been denied an honorable death on the battlefield like his ancestors.

During a hurricane, Lieutenant Dan straps himself to the mast in defiance and rages at God! He curses God and says it's time they had it out once and for all.

As the storm subsides, Lieutenant Dan finds acceptance, thanking Forrest for saving his life before jumping overboard to swim in the calm waters. I like this scene because it shows the transformative power of acceptance and how it can help heal pain, grief and anger, enabling us to move forward.

Grief is a universal experience, yet we all experience it differently. Recently, a friend shared a realization following his divorce—thanks to his counselor—that while he was beginning to grieve the end of his marriage, his wife had already processed this loss five years earlier.

As difficult as grief can be, we all have the strength to overcome it. Progress is possible through gratitude, integrity, and kindness. These can be the true healing balms for your pain. Be patient with yourself; it's not a cycle to get through. It will happen when it happens. Take care of yourself.

LIFE HACKS

When it comes to grief, there's no silver bullet or quick fix. The suggestions below are ways you can support yourself while experiencing grief.

MINDFULNESS

❖ ACKNOWLEDGE IT: Grief is real, natural, and takes time to work through. Acknowledging it to yourself and others can be difficult because society tells us to buck up and not complain. Remember, grief is not complaining. It's a legitimate feeling. You may want to try a meditation practice around your grief.

JOURNALING

❖ WRITE A LETTER: In your journal, you may want to write a letter to a person you've lost or someone who has hurt or harmed you. Share what you're feeling—the pain, shame, anger, sadness, frustration, gratitude, etc. Let them know what you plan to do to keep living, find your strength, and carry on.

ACTIONS

❖ ASK FOR SUPPORT: This can be as simple as asking a friend to help or yelling and screaming about it with someone there. Ask for help and let others support you.

❖ CRY: Crying is a good thing. As I get older, I allow myself to cry more. It's cathartic to cry and let out your emotions when you're sad or grieving. Find a friend or loved one who can sit with you and just be there when you cry and grieve.

5

ANGER

I SPEND A LOT OF time thinking about anger. I come from a long line of family members who anger quickly. Like many in my family, I am extroverted, so I wear my emotions and feelings on my sleeve. I get passionate at times and can get heated in discussions. I don't get angry very often, but when I do, I can say things without thinking. Fortunately, I'm also quick to apologize and/or forgive, but being careful with my words is one of the things I have to work on.

Anger is a natural and often adaptive emotion that can motivate us to take action, assert ourselves, or set boundaries when we feel threatened or wronged. However, when anger is not managed properly, it can be highly destructive, both to ourselves and others.

Some of the common causes of anger include:

❖ Being threatened or treated unfairly;

❖ Being publicly humiliated or having your self-esteem or confidence undermined in public;

- ❖ Personal problems such as financial stress or stress at work;
- ❖ Past experiences;
- ❖ Trauma/abuse;
- ❖ Bereavement and grief;
- ❖ Existing mental health conditions.

I like this diagram, which shows feelings that can lead to anger. Often, when I feel angry, it's because of some underlying emotion.

Feelings That Lead to Anger

Many things can trigger my anger, such as reckless drivers, someone cutting me off in traffic without seeming to care. In the past, I used to respond by honking the horn for longer than necessary or speeding up to tailgate them while honking. I was frustrated because my expectations about driving with courtesy and respect were violated, leading to anger. However, I'm actively working on improving this aspect of myself. While I don't claim to be a perfect driver and still occasionally lose my cool, I'm much better than I used to be. I try not to let my frustration turn to anger.

Living in Spain and Portugal for a year helped me with this. Here, like many other countries around the world, driving is, well, just another part of daily life. For instance, on a busy five-lane round-about, it's common for someone to abruptly change four lanes right in front of you without signaling. The expected perception isn't that they are in the wrong. Instead, you're expected to avoid hitting them. They obviously had a reason for doing it, and it's okay. Blaring your horn isn't a solution; just slow down and continue on your way. If you encounter a truck stopped on a narrow lane to unload, you wait patiently without honking. You wait and relax—it's all good. At first, I found this lack of respect for my time insulting, but I slowly realized that these people weren't intentionally targeting me; I was not their focus. They were going somewhere; I was going somewhere. We would all get to where we were going, albeit a few minutes later than expected. Over time, I shifted my focus away from reacting in frustration and anger, realizing that it robbed me of peace. Now, when I'm back in the US or Australia, I just smile, try to maintain a relaxed attitude, and go with the flow.

You don't need to move to Spain to adopt this shift in perspective. It's more about identifying the root cause of our anger and addressing it. Sometimes, removing ourselves from situations or people who trigger our anger can help, but this isn't always feasible.

Have you noticed that people seem to be getting angrier faster and more frequently? Whether it's road rage or encounters with others, many of us seem to be constantly on edge, ready to explode at the slightest provocation. I see videos daily of someone on a plane, in a car, in a store, or just walking down the road being angry with someone else. I refer to this as "speed anger," in which we instantly react defensively because our pride, identity, or sense of entitlement feels threatened. Perhaps we feel humiliated, shamed, ignored, scared, or hurt.

Regardless of the cause, this anger often simmers beneath the surface, waiting to be unleashed by any minor trigger. I've found that if I stop and take time to reflect on the situation and understand what's being said, I often realize there's no need to be angry. The challenge lies in stopping and reflecting, something I sometimes do well and other times struggle with. However, I've found that if I deal with my anger by talking it through, writing about it, or processing it somehow, it helps to prevent it from lingering. It usually fades away, replaced by other matters that require my attention or energy.

Responsibility for anger

My wife receives a daily email from DailyStoic.com, which delves into the philosophy of Stoicism and Marcus Aurelius and discusses how to apply these principles to everyday life. We often read the emails together and have great discussions about stoicism.

One aspect of stoicism I particularly like is its emphasis on taking responsibility for our response to anger. Whether we choose to react with calmness or agitation, the decision ultimately lies with us.

I enjoy delving into the meaning of words. Responsibility means having the ability to respond. It's important to remember this concept when dealing with anger. How are we able to respond to anger? Our choices are among our fundamental abilities as humans. Do we choose to respond to anger with more anger, especially when we feel slighted or treated unfairly? Do we choose anger in the face of perceived injustice, seeking to overpower and destroy others to assert dominance? Anger, like fear, can serve as a powerful motivator, triggering our fight, flight, or freeze response. Philosophies like Stoicism encourage us to pause, take a breath, and ask questions before reacting.

It seems we're becoming conditioned to get angry more quickly. Perhaps it's due to our online culture or a growing belief that "I" matters more than others. Whatever the cause, anger seems to be increasingly used daily as a rallying cry around issues that should unite us but instead divide us. This trend saddens and frustrates me, and yes, it even makes me angry. However, I must remind myself that I'm responsible for my own actions and their impact on others.

Think about the things that provoke anger in you. Do they distance you from your friends and family? Do they create divisions between you and your neighbors, isolating you from your community? If so, I challenge you to find alternative outlets for your emotions besides anger. Pause, take a breath, and reflect before reacting. Remember, we are not slaves to our emotions; we control them. I'm not saying we shouldn't feel angry; that's impossible. What I am saying is that we need to be aware of how our anger affects us and those around us.

I used to hang out with people who were angry often, which stressed me and made me angry as well. Realizing that they affected my own demeanor, I gradually chose to distance myself from those people, and I am glad I did. The distance provided me with perspective.

We live in a chaotic world where anger is prevalent. Anger is a potent emotion; it can make us feel empowered, especially in response to situations that disempower us.

For most of us, anger is a normal emotion we learn to manage. However, for some, anger can pose a more serious problem. If you frequently become angry or struggle to control your anger, and if it leads to lashing out at others or violence, you may want to reach out for support. While anger may initially provide a sense of empowerment, it is short-lived and can harm our health. The aftermath of a brief angry outburst can significantly impact the person it is directed at. You may feel better by releasing the anger, but the other person may take longer to recover from your anger. In these cases, I have found that it takes some listening and forgiveness to repair the relationship.

Story: Five Angry Women

A friend shared a story about a couple who had been together for about a decade and owned a home and a business together. When the wife discovered her husband's year-long affair with a younger woman, she was devastated and kicked him out. He temporarily lived in his van, leaving most of his belongings behind while he looked for a place to live.

In the weeks after he left, the wife's friends rallied around her. One evening, a group of the wife's friends came over for a few drinks— my friend being one of them. The evening began with some fun and laughter. Fueled by drinks and emotions, they decided to pack up the husband's belongings to spare the wife from seeing them. However, things took a dark turn when someone grabbed scissors and started destroying his belongings. This kicked off an evening of angry destruction. What began as outrage toward this one man and revenge for the woman soon escalated into a mob mentality, with each woman unleashing pent-up anger, not just toward the husband, but toward other men who had harmed or wronged them. That night, these five angry women cut up most of his clothes, defaced his paintings, and pretty much destroyed anything of his they could find. My friend said the anger was palatable.

The next day, my friend woke up feeling ashamed of herself, as did some of the other women involved. She couldn't believe she had participated in these actions, which were unlike her. She spoke with some of the other women who were there that night, and they felt the same way. What had come over them for them to manifest this collective outpouring of unresolved anger and hurt?

I've reflected on this story quite a bit. There's a lot to unpack, but here are my main takeaways:

❖ These women's anger was genuine and rooted in past hurt, frustration, shame, rejection, and/or humiliation.

❖ Their anger led them to destroy this man's possessions, which was a behavior they all regretted afterward.

❖ While their anger was real and justified, their actions were not.

Remember, anger is a normal emotion, and it's okay to feel it. Still, what we need to take note of is how we express and manage that anger. Learning to handle anger constructively can lead to healthier relationships, improved mental and physical wellbeing, and a more fulfilling life.

LIFE HACKS
Here are some ideas on ways to deal with anger healthily.

JOURNALING
In your journal, spend some time reflecting on when you get angry. Describe the situations and feelings you have. Try to identify what causes you to get angry. Knowing your triggers or underlying causes can help you anticipate and manage your reactions.

ACTIONS
THINK BEFORE YOU SPEAK: When you feel anger rising, take a deep breath to calm your body's stress response. Count to ten before reacting to give yourself and the other people involved a chance to think before you respond and say something you may regret later.

COMMUNICATE: Express your feelings calmly and assertively, using "I" statements to describe your emotions without blaming others. Effective communication can help resolve conflicts you may be having with others.

TIMEOUTS: If you feel overwhelmed by anger, remove yourself from the situation temporarily. Go for a walk, listen to music, or engage in an activity that calms you down.

6

EXTERNAL CHAOS

ANY DISCUSSION OF CHAOS IN our lives would be incomplete without exploring the external factors that fuel it. Things like trauma, conflict, grief, and toxic people are part of the human experience; we've all dealt with them at some point in our lives—often multiple times. Some of us may be grappling with them right now.

External chaos isn't something we invite into our lives; it usually arrives unannounced courtesy of other people and unforeseen events. How we react to this chaos varies, but it usually involves a mix of grief and anger. If we respond in anger with thoughts of vengeance or lashing out, we risk becoming agents of chaos ourselves, spreading turmoil to those around us.

Dealing with external chaos is never easy. It can affect us physically, psychologically, and emotionally, sometimes all at once. Its impact can be profound, shaping our lives and the way we relate to others. In the following chapters, I'll explore how external chaos can impact our lives and connections with others.

7

TRAUMA

TRAUMA IS AN OFTEN-USED term today, and there is a plethora of resources like books, expert interviews, discussion groups, and podcasts dedicated to the topic. Simply put, trauma is the emotional aftermath of a distressing, frightening, or stressful event, which can occur as a single incident or over time. Trauma can impact a person's sense of safety, self, and ability to regulate emotions and navigate relationships.

It feels like there's an epidemic of trauma in today's world, and there are two reasons for this. Firstly, we talk about trauma more openly now compared to a decade or two ago. Social media may be one reason for this. People see others talking about trauma and can identify with their stories. Secondly, our understanding of trauma has grown significantly, recognizing its profound effect on mental health and life in general.

Trauma is a fundamental source of external chaos. While many of us encounter trauma at some point, not everyone reacts similarly to it. Most people can recover with support from loved ones and professional help, but for others, trauma can lead to ongoing physical and mental health challenges.

Childhood trauma

Childhood trauma—often referred to as Adverse Childhood Experiences (ACEs)—can greatly impact a child's physical and mental health, which can carry on into adulthood. These traumatic experiences range from abuse and neglect to growing up in homes of violence and substance abuse. The younger a child is when they experience this trauma, the greater its impact. Plus, there's a direct link between the number of traumatic events a child experiences and their behavior, mental health, and physical health down the road.

Many of us have experienced trauma as kids, and its effects can stay with us for life. If we don't recognize this trauma and address it, it can manifest into negative behaviors as an adult. Healing from childhood trauma often takes a lot of time and support.

In the early '90s, I worked with a summer camp program for kids from a tough neighborhood in Washington, DC. One of my coworkers from New Zealand was floored by how every kid seemed to know someone in their neighborhood who had died, often due to violence or drugs. In many cases, these were family members. I can't help but wonder how all that trauma affected those kids as they grew up.

Adult trauma

In a world of external chaos, trauma seems to be all around us at every stage of our lives. As adults, many of us face trauma—physical, sexual, or emotional abuse, accidents, terrorism, or natural disasters. The stats are pretty staggering—most American adults have faced trauma at some point in their lives. Violence, especially from intimate partners, affects many people, and sexual assault is also common for both adults and children.

When people experience trauma, they sometimes turn to dangerous behaviors to cope—substance use, self-harm, or risky sexual behavior. It's not a healthy way to deal with the emotional pain, but it can feel like a way to regain control or numb the pain, at least temporarily.

Experiencing trauma, especially in childhood, can lead to feelings of low self-worth, anxiety, and a need for control, which can contribute to developing mental health issues like eating disorders.

I remember a conversation I had with my daughter some time ago about trauma. She said, "Dad, trauma sucks!" She experienced trauma herself. When she was nine, her mother and I divorced. The divorce was far from cordial. It was litigious, and despite our best intentions to not put our kids on the firing line, we used them as pawns in the games we played. Fear and anxiety became constant companions for my daughter, leading her to develop an eating disorder. This disorder, described to me as a voice of self-hatred, plagued her with feelings of inadequacy.

She wrestled with her eating disorder for years, all while experiencing social isolation at school and the typical struggles of teenage life, which only increased her anxiety and depression. As a parent, I often felt powerless—like I was merely watching from the sidelines. Any parent who has seen their child struggle with mental health issues can relate to this feeling.

Today, my daughter works as a social worker. Through tremendous effort and professional support, she reclaimed her sense of self. She is now confident, kind, creative, and strong. Yet, like many of us, she still wrestles with the lingering effects of trauma, fear, and anxiety. These challenges may never disappear completely, but she has learned to navigate them.

Recovery and support

It's important to remember that everyone reacts to trauma differently. Some people are more resilient, and others have access to professional help. Early intervention, an understanding of trauma, and supportive relationships can make a big difference for people trying to heal. Remember, our trauma does not define us. It can be significant and impact our lives, but it is not who we are.

Impact of trauma

Living through traumatic events can be, well, traumatic. Trauma packs a punch, both emotionally and physically. Here's what you may experience:

EMOTIONALLY

❖ Numbness: Like your emotions are on mute. This is a common shock response.

❖ Anger: Trauma can leave you frustrated, even rageful. It's okay to feel it, but to have healthy outlets.

❖ Anxiety: Feeling constantly on edge, jumpy, or worried? That's your body's alarm system in high gear.

❖ Guilt: Trauma can trick you into blaming yourself, even if it wasn't your fault. Remember, you're not to blame.

❖ Sadness: Feeling low, discouraged, or even hopeless is normal. Still, know that this darkness won't last forever.

❖ Confusion: The world may feel upside down, leaving you unsure of what's real. It's okay to be confused, and seeking help may clear the fog.

PHYSICALLY

❖ Fatigue: Feeling constantly drained? Trauma can leave you running on fumes.

❖ Concentration crumbles: Focusing feels impossible, like your brain can't hold it together.

❖ Appetite fluctuations: Sometimes, it disappears, and other times, it goes on overdrive. Both are coping mechanisms, but healthy eating habits help.

❖ Sleep inconsistencies: Insomnia plagues your nights, or you can't get out of bed? Sleep disturbances are common, but developing healthy sleep habits can help.

❖ Blood pressure spikes: Feeling your heart race or chest tighten? Trauma can affect your blood pressure, but stress management helps.

Trauma is common, but it doesn't have to define you. With support and understanding, you can heal and move forward.

Story: Living And Flourishing Despite Trauma

A friend of mine named Amanda has had a lifetime of trauma. When she was nine, her father left. Her mother had to take care of her and her two brothers, and she soon found a new partner who moved into the family home. However, this man was physically and emotionally abusive to the mother and kids. One day, after a particularly bad beating, he locked Amanda, her mom, and siblings in a closet, only to reappear a few hours later with a shotgun, threatening to pull the trigger and leave the children without a mother. This cycle went on for a few years. They left a few times, but Amanda's mother would always return, putting the children back in harm's way.

Later in life, Amanda married, and although not physically abusive, her husband was emotionally abusive. He was a bully and a narcissist. When their marriage fell apart, her young children became weapons in his war against her. After separating, she went to pick up the kids from school one afternoon and was told that their father had taken them out of school early. She tried to call her ex, but he wouldn't answer. She went by his house, but the house was empty. The police refused to get involved as she told them she didn't think he would harm the children. Two weeks later, her ex called and said if she wanted to see her kids again, she'd have to sign over her rights to everything (property, investments, etc.) to him.

For many agonizing months, she was separated from her kids. After signing the legal documents, she was reunited with her children. It turned out that her children and ex had been staying with Amanda's mother the whole time. Her ex had convinced her mother that Amanda had joined a cult and that the children needed to be protected from her. Amanda's deeply religious mother believed the lies and didn't tell Amanda she knew where her children were.

I'm happy to say Amanda now has a wonderful relationship with her adult children and is in a great relationship with a man who loves her. She is happy and finds joy in life! An artist, a scholar, and someone with friends who love her, she is one of the coolest people I've ever known.

I often reflect on Amanda's journey. As a parent myself, I can't fathom the pain of having my children taken from me. I can only imagine the trauma, fear, and grief she must have experienced. Her resilience in the face of such trauma is awe-inspiring. Amanda is one of those people who, despite the trauma she has experienced, loves. She loves her family and her friends—she loves herself, and she loves life!

While most people will experience trauma in their life, not everyone will be traumatized by it. Trauma isn't a life sentence. People can and do recover and go on to live their best life. Remember, healing after trauma takes time and patience. Be gentle with yourself, celebrate your progress, and don't hesitate to seek professional help if you need it.

LIFE HACKS
Here are some strategies that can help manage stress and support healing after traumatic events:

Journaling
One effective journaling technique for coping with trauma is Expressive Journaling, created by neuroscientist Dr. James Pennebaker. This method can lead to emotional relief, clearer thinking, and improved overall wellbeing. You can find information on the specifics of this practice online.

ACTIONS

❖ Talking: Talking to someone you trust and sharing your experience with them can be incredibly helpful.

❖ Getting help: A therapist can offer personalized guidance and support to help you deal with the trauma.

❖ Physical activity: Plan and participate in regular physical activity. This can release endorphins, improve mood, and boost your energy levels. Find activities you enjoy, like walking, swimming, hiking, or dancing.

❖ Sleeping: Prioritize getting enough quality sleep by establishing a regular sleep schedule, creating a relaxing bedtime routine, and avoiding screens before going to bed.

❖ Mindful eating: Focus on nutritious foods that fuel your body and mind. Avoid using substances like alcohol and/or drugs to cope, as they can worsen symptoms in the long run.

❖ Being creative: Engaging in activities you enjoy, like art, music, writing, or spending time in nature, can be a healthy way to process emotions and express yourself.

8

CONFLICT

SOMEONE ONCE TOLD ME THAT conflict resulted from people having differences about significant things. For example, when your values, principles, norms, motivations, perceptions, ideas, or desires are challenged, disagreed with, or attacked by others, conflict can occur.

Conflict is a natural part of life. Some of us like conflict, and others shy away from it. Our personality, how we were raised, our environment, and our relationships all play a part in how we perceive, participate in, and deal with conflict.

In today's world of chaos, conflict seems to be a new spectator sport. For instance, a friend of mine enjoys watching YouTube videos in which individuals, often referred to as "Karens," unexpectedly confront others over seemingly trivial matters. Let's be honest, many of us enjoy watching a good argument from the sidelines, sometimes finding humor in it. We may try to make light of the situation, but for many of us, conflict is uncomfortable.

I've always had an affinity for history, especially the tales that shaped our nation. One group that's captivated my interest is the Cherokee people. Divided after the Trail of Tears, the Eastern Band of Cherokee now calls Western North Carolina home. I've visited Cherokee a few times, exploring the museum and hiking the surrounding national forests.

One aspect of Cherokee history that fascinates me is how they organized their towns into red (war) territories and white (peace) territories, each governed by a respective chief—a Peace Chief or a War Chief. The Peace Chief handled domestic affairs and ceremonies during peacetime, while the War Chief managed alliances and led during war or conflict. Interestingly, even during peace times, the War Chiefs kept their warriors prepared, focusing on training and diplomacy.

I admire how the Cherokee approached conflict, recognizing the diverse roles within their tribe. It's intriguing to see how War Chiefs could spend years without engaging in battle, instead focusing on diplomacy and building alliances. Both red and white territories and their chiefs had different functions, yet they shared a common goal: the wellbeing and continuity of their people. This historical example resonates today, reminding me of conflict resolution's multifaceted nature. Even in modern military training, soldiers learn not only combat but also negotiation and coalition-building skills.

As we experience conflict in our own lives, we have opportunities to get a different outcome by staying cool and positive.

Understanding our role in conflict

Similar to the Cherokee, it's important to think about our actions and roles when facing conflict. Most of us instinctively play to our strengths and personalities when in conflict. Some may confront the issue head-on, while others prefer to step back and fight another day. We may also try to negotiate a settlement or outcome.

I was raised never to back down, particularly if the cause is just, then the understanding was you fight. However, this inclination toward conflict has been a double-edged sword for me. While I've fought hard for what I believe in, I've also realized the emotional toll it can take on others. This is something I've been examining over the past couple of years. How can I address conflict with others while maintaining integrity? Is it possible to reach a resolution without causing harm? By taking time to think about my role in conflict and how it may affect others, I have an opportunity to respond to conflict differently. I can choose to negotiate or walk away as opposed to fighting. It's very liberating when you try different strategies, ones that may lead to the outcome being different, unexpected, or even better.

Win/win

Let's consider the concept of win/win. While it's often discussed, achieving true win/win outcomes is rare. As a society, we often prioritize the win-at-all-costs mindset, but I've come to see that it's not practical for life and relationships. Having a win/lose mentality is a zero-sum proposition that typically ends up hurting both sides.

Win/win does not necessarily mean that both parties walk away with what they want; rather, they agree on an outcome they can both live with. Because of this, win/win resolutions tend to last longer than others. To make a win/win situation work, both parties must be:

- ❖ Willing to negotiate honestly and sincerely;
- ❖ Aware of each other's needs and desire to get an outcome for all;
- ❖ Open to compromise on their own positions for the sake of a mutually beneficial outcome.

So, what happens if you can't reach a win/win? What happens if the other party refuses to negotiate in good faith? Then, you either fight, accept the situation, or leave (I'll talk more about these choices later).

Story: Andy And Ellen's Non-Traditional Wedding

Andy and Ellen had been together for ten years and decided to tie the knot in a way that reflected their values. For them, it wasn't about pomp and circumstance but bringing their friends and family together for a joyful celebration.

Their wedding plans included music, dancing, great local beers and wines, delicious food (including North Carolina pulled pork, for which I had the honor of being the pitmaster!), and a unique twist: they would exchange vows privately on a mountain top on the day of the wedding. Legal formalities would follow with a registrar a couple of weeks after the wedding.

However, not everyone was thrilled. The groom's father and the bride's mother voiced strong opposition. "How can you have a wedding without a minister?" "It's not a real wedding if it's not officiated," "What will your grandparents think?" they argued, causing a lot of hurt and frustration. Despite the pressure, the couple held their ground. They explained that this was what they wanted and set boundaries. They told the parents that they were welcome to come and celebrate, but it was no longer up for discussion.

Andy and Ellen confronted the conflict head-on, refusing to compromise their wishes. And you know what? Their wedding was everything they dreamed of. The parents joined in the celebration and kept any reservations to themselves.

This story illustrates a key lesson: conflicts often arise from differing expectations. Andy and Ellen's vision didn't align with their parents' traditional views, but they navigated the disagreement with grace and determination. I admire the way Andy and Ellen handled the situation, mainly because, in the end, they got a win.

LIFE HACKS
Conflict can be tough. Here are some things I think about when I'm in conflict:

JOURNALING & MINDFULNESS
❖ DOES IT MATTER? The first thing I do is to ask myself if this matters to me and why. Sometimes, I realize it doesn't really matter, or it doesn't matter enough to enter the fray. Then, I work on letting it go. As we'll explore later, leaving is one of my most powerful choices. However, if I decide it does matter to me, then how do I proceed in a way that retains my integrity and values?

❖ IT'S ABOUT THE OUTCOME. Next, I ask myself what outcome I want or need. Identifying what I can live with may be the best outcome. This may require me to negotiate or walk away/let it go. After all, you must choose your battles, as not every battle is worth fighting.

❖ NEGOTIATE BY UNDERSTANDING. The other thing I try to do is understand what's important to the other person. Often, I find that we care about the same thing. I can let go of my need to score points or have a win. Even if it can be hard to do and takes practice, showing I'm willing to listen and trying to understand can diffuse much of the conflict. What also truly helps is trying to imagine stepping out of the conflict, asking questions, and practicing active listening.

9

TOXIC PEOPLE

ONE OF MY FAVORITE PIECES of advice from my mother was, "Stay away from the Devil, deep water, and Christian plumbers." Now, before any Christians, plumbers, or Christian plumbers get mad, let me explain.

The Devil is straightforward—stay away to avoid pain and harm. Deep water can be treacherous, and we can quickly get overwhelmed and drown. Christian plumbers is a bit more nuanced. My mom's point was based on her experiences of being scammed, hurt, or taken advantage of by people who proclaimed they were moral, good Christians or Christian-like, but their actions told a different story. Having experienced people like this, I know how difficult this situation can be.

If you've encountered sociopaths, psychopaths, or narcissists, you've met toxicity. Toxic people consistently harm others through their actions—intentional or not—often through emotional manipulation. However, it's important to point out that not all toxic people fit these clinical definitions. Many exhibit toxic behaviors unknowingly, or worse, they justify them through some belief: moral, religious, political, or legal. The bottom line is that if you've been manipulated, harmed, or abused by another person, they were being toxic.

So, what are the signs of toxic people? I've listed different types to look out for, understanding that they may exhibit all or just a few of these traits:

❖ EMOTIONAL GAMERS: These people use manipulation, passive-aggressive behavior, and emotional blackmail to obtain what they want. Their verbal attacks and insults are usually passive-aggressive. They often use negative humor to get a reaction out of you. They may withhold affection or punish you for no reason.

❖ GASLIGHTERS: These clever people are the ones who paint you with a negative brush without owning their part in the process or relationship. They use emotional manipulation to sow doubt in your mind. They use fear to bring on allies and watch them pile on. When you're at the bottom of the pile, you end up wondering what you did wrong, hint: probably nothing. Their toxic behavior is not your fault. We often see this behavior on social media, in the workplace, and in our interpersonal lives.

❖ ARTFUL DODGERS: These toxic people avoid the truth, and accountability. They try to avoid conflict, seeing it as something to fear and avoid. The challenge here is that they usually leave without an explanation or a resolution.

❖ OUT-OF-BOUNDS PLAYERS: These are the people who do not respect boundaries. They trample on them, ignore them, and make up their own rules to suit their own goals and objectives. The problem is they're always playing with a stacked deck. If you work or live with an out-of-bounds player, beware—they're out to win, and you will lose.

❖ EMOTIONAL VAMPIRES: These people emotionally drain your energy just by being around. They are constantly negative, sucking light and joy out of a room and people's lives. I have known a few of these people, and they are difficult to be around. I always envision the dementors from Harry Potter when dealing with emotional vampires.

❖ POWER PLAYERS: These people see the world in black and white and are masters at power dynamics. Winning and power are their drugs. The more they accumulate, the more they justify their power. They can quickly see weakness—real or perceived—and exploit it. In business, I've encountered many of these people. Having clear expectations and legal contracts can help but do not guarantee success.

❖ TRAUMA MERCHANTS: These are people who use fear, anger, and trauma to motivate others for their own gain. I often think of politicians or evangelist preachers who wield trauma as a weapon for their personal wealth or gain, laughing to themselves as they fly off on their private jets to the next rally, presentation, or event.

❖ OUTRAGE DEALERS: We seem to get outraged so easily these days. Outrage dealers are clever at using outrage as a rallying cry to divide and drive a wedge into relationships and people's lives. Think of the families and communities who've become fractured over political or social issues. We're becoming more divided, and outrage dealers are there to sow the seeds and fan the flames.

❖ SITH LORDS OF TOXICITY: I'm a Star Wars fan, so please indulge me here. The Sith Lords in the Star Wars mythology were masters of the dark side of the force who used trauma, fear, anger, and hate to increase their power. These toxic people are the Darth Vaders of our lives. They can move between the toxic traits described above with ease, often combining them to hurt others.

I realize this is pretty negative. However, from my experience and those of my friends, family, and colleagues, I know toxic people exist, and they do real damage to people's lives. One of the paradoxes of toxicity is that we can all engage in toxic behaviors at times, me included.

Story: The Toxic Card Game

A few years ago, my wife, her daughter, my son, and I were playing a game of cards. We're all competitive, and Australia has a great culture of "sledging" in sports, in which competitors will slag off members of the other team before or during a game to gain an emotional advantage.

At the beginning of the card game, there was some good verbal back and forth and banter, but as the evening wore on, it turned ugly. The situation escalated when my son and I turned our fun sledging into something more personal. The focus of our attacks was my wife's daughter. At one point, my son looked at me, wanting to know if what we were doing was okay. I didn't say anything. My non-verbal response was, "Yeah, go for it." Finally, my wife said, "Enough!"

Afterward, I felt really bad. I'd used ugly language and dropped emotional bombs; I'd been toxic. What's worse, I'd been complacent in my son's behavior. We both apologized, and now, when we play games, I strive to be more aware of my behavior.

When I reflect on that night, I think our behavior was a form of one-upmanship, in which someone dares to go beyond what's acceptable, and there's no consequence. This can make the next person do the same thing or go a little further until, eventually, you're engaged in something completely unacceptable or out of control. Then, when you're called out on it or later reflect, you can't believe you participated.

I could blame my behavior that night on past trauma, but I was the one there that night. I chose to behave the way I did. I also could have justified my behavior and made excuses by pointing out that the fault was in how my wife's daughter reacted—in other words, blame the victim. I could have said, "Well, it's just a game, and she shouldn't get so upset." However, being aware means you check your own behavior. It means you don't rationalize or make excuses for toxicity in yourself or others.

Now, I don't believe I'm a toxic person as I strive to be aware of my behavior, to learn from it, and to change. Most toxic people are either completely unaware they're being toxic, or they're fully aware and choose not to change their behavior.

Toxic enablers

Toxic people don't exist in a vacuum. They have victims, but what's worse, they also have enablers. Enablers, by their position and viewpoint, are more aware of the toxic person's behavior and see first-hand the results; however, they choose to allow and enable the behavior. Maybe this is due to some form of codependency. Perhaps it's a survival instinct, or they benefit from that person, so they don't want to call them out on their behavior. For whatever reason, they enable toxic behavior. Many of us have been guilty of this in our own lives. As stated in the story above, I enabled my son and allowed behavior I knew was wrong and hurtful. I also joined in.

True enablers adopt this role as a full-time vocation. They're masters at clearing space for toxic people to be toxic. They make excuses for the toxic person and run interference, often showing empathy to the victims. Frequently, this can compound the toxicity as the empathy is not authentic, and the interference and excuses become toxic as well. I've seen this in many relationships in which one person is toxic, and the other person enables that toxicity.

Story: The Toxic Doc And His Crew Of Enablers

Several years ago I met a prominent doctor, a leader in his field. He worked with me on an advisory board, and we developed a good relationship. I met his family and we decided to launch a business together. We hired his wife and adult son to be a part of the business too.

A few months after the business launched, I started experiencing his form of toxicity firsthand. He was a trauma merchant, an artful dodger, and a liar. He also had a cast of enablers, from family members to colleagues and friends. They ran interference for him, often hiding or covering up the results of his behavior. They also benefited from his success. Chief among his enablers was his son. Although he was usually the target of his father's bullying and abuse, he witnessed his father's toxic behavior toward others and chose to look the other way. The doctor's wife was also an enabler, making excuses and turning a blind eye to the way he treated others. Some of his business colleagues also ignored the behavior as they benefited from his celebrity.

I found out I wasn't the first person to experience the doctor's toxicity. His toxic behavior had left several former business partners and stakeholders disillusioned and angry.

The people who enabled him demonstrated that their own self-interests outweighed their stated values. In the second part of this book, I talk about powerful choices. One of these is to leave. Ultimately, I chose to walk away from the toxic doc, and his crew. Their values and behaviors did not align with mine. It was a painful process, but for my own wellbeing, I had to let go, and I'm glad I did.

Toxic paradox

One of the paradoxes I wrestle with is when toxic people also do good. This makes me wonder: does their toxicity outweigh their good deeds? I guess it depends on where you sit. If you benefit from their good work, you may view them as a hero, but if you're one of their victims, you may view them as a villain. We're all complex; however, if people are toxic and aware of their behavior yet refuse to change, then I err on the side of "Screw them!" This may not be right, and forgiveness may be the healthier route, but it's how I often feel.

The toxic doc is a great example of this. Even though he's a toxic person, he's also a doctor who has helped many. This presents a challenge for me. I've witnessed and experienced his toxic behavior firsthand, yet some people see him as heroic. I know I cannot change or fix him. I tried holding up a mirror to him, but he was disinterested in hearing feedback or changing. Ultimately, this is his journey, not mine. All I can do is warn people to be careful, so they don't get hurt by the trauma he inflicts.

This also says a lot about human nature. I'm not here to judge others. How do I know what's in other people's hearts? I have to believe that toxic people are not necessarily bad, especially when I see them do good things to help others. The challenge is that their toxicity often overshadows the good they do.

Dealing with toxic people can be difficult, and there are a few things we can do to deal with them effectively. Remember, they're better at this than we are. Recognize that they have the power when you engage with them, so avoid fighting them directly. Make yourself unavailable or leave the situation if you can. If you must engage with them, limit your time. Give yourself some space and a buffer against them, so you can recompose, reorder, and refocus.

LIFE HACKS

If you choose to or must deal with toxic people, I've found helpful ways of doing that:

ACTIONS

GREY ROCKING: This is also referred to as "grey rock" or "grey stone." It allows us to engage in conversation with toxic people without being sucked into their games or toxicity. Imagine you're a big grey rock out in the woods. The toxic person tries to engage you, goat you, or lure you in, but you are just there. Simple ways to do this include avoiding eye contact and not offering them any information they can weaponize against you. If possible, communicate with them virtually rather than in person. Grey rocking requires us to practice the art of indifference. This doesn't mean you don't care; it just means you are indifferent to their tactics.

Here are some examples of grey rocking:

❖ Answer questions vaguely and with one-word.

❖ Don't volunteer information about yourself, your friends, or your family. This will limit the areas that toxic people can exploit.

❖ Don't apologize, explain, or make excuses for yourself. Remember, you're not acting in a toxic manner; they are.

❖ Don't engage in conversation. If they engage, then limit conversations to a minimum.

FOCUS ON THE OUTCOME: One of my favorite hacks for dealing with toxic people is to ask, "What outcome do you want?" When they're doing their thing, I've found that this simple question can disarm a situation and redirect their toxic behavior. Most of the time, it removes you as the target and refocuses their behavior back on them. Try it.

MINDFULNESS
BREATHING: I find when I'm dealing with toxic people that breathing helps. I use the 1-2-3 breathing exercise. Start to count silently forward (1, 2, 3) as you inhale, then backward (3, 2, 1) as you exhale. Gradually make each exhalation twice as long as each inhalation. Focus on breathing slowly and smoothly, humming each time you exhale. There are other breathing

exercises out there, and I encourage you to find one that works for you.

JOURNALING

I've found that when I deal with toxic people, their toxicity can linger. Journaling about the experience helps me process it and let go. Here are some questions you may explore while journaling:

❖ What happened? Describe the interaction and the person's toxic behavior.

❖ What was my response?

❖ What was the outcome?

❖ What are my next steps?

I've used the hacks above with success. Note that toxicity can have a real and lasting impact on our mental health and self-esteem, so asking for help if you're dealing with a toxic person is fine.

10

OPPORTUNITIES CHAOS CAN BRING TO OUR LIVES

EXPERIENCING CHAOS FROM EXTERNAL SOURCES, such as trauma, conflict, and toxic people, can be incredibly distressing. Similarly, dealing with internal chaos, including feelings of fear, anxiety, grief, and anger, can be overwhelming. Symptoms like depression, suicidal thoughts, loneliness, isolation, abuse, and neglect often accompany chaos, negatively impacting our wellbeing. As the chaos intensifies, it can erode our self-worth, leaving us vulnerable and even paralyzed.

Chaos also affects our relationships, eroding trust and making it harder to navigate connections with others. These challenges are a daily reality for many, often unavoidable and resistant to simple solutions. The complexity of chaos contributes to its destructive nature, leaving us wondering how to protect our mental, physical, and emotional wellbeing.

By living in the *all-is-well* mindset, we can begin to build resilience and confront the chaos in our lives. By doing so, we can gradually reclaim our best selves and live our best lives. In the second half of this book, we will explore strategies to navigate chaos more effectively. Still, here are some approaches that help me when I'm experiencing chaos:

❖ MINDFULNESS AND SELF-AWARENESS: Practicing mindfulness techniques, such as deep breathing, journaling, yoga, meditation, and spending time in nature, helps me to stay grounded in the present moment. This enables me to observe my thoughts and emotions without judgment, gaining insight into the chaos I'm experiencing and managing my reactions more effectively.

❖ CHALLENGING NEGATIVE THOUGHTS: I consciously try to stop and analyze my internal dialogue in response to the chaos I'm experiencing. Is it empowering and supportive, or does it undermine and discourage me? If it's negative, I work on challenging and silencing these harmful thoughts, recognizing that they hinder rather than help me.

❖ SETTING REALISTIC GOALS: When experiencing chaos, I try to set attainable goals to move through or away from the turmoil. I find that breaking down larger goals into smaller, manageable steps and achieving these steps can boost my confidence and reduce the stress that chaos causes.

❖ FOCUSING ON CONTROLLABLE FACTORS: Acknowledging that I can't control everything allows me to direct my energy toward what I can influence, letting go of the rest. This shift in focus empowers me to channel my efforts and energy to where they can make a difference, yielding tangible results.

❖ VISUALIZATION: Imagining myself successfully confronting, overcoming, or letting go of the chaos can help me build confidence and reduce anxiety. What does it look like when I'm through to the other side? Visualization is a powerful tool that allows us to mentally prepare for and navigate challenging situations.

❖ SEEKING SUPPORT: Sharing my thoughts, feelings, fears and stress with someone I trust provides validation and encouragement. Whether confiding in friends, family, or a mental health professional, seeking support is essential for coping with chaos.

❖ COGNITIVE-BEHAVIORAL THERAPY (CBT): This evidence-based approach can help identify and change negative thought patterns and behaviors associated with chaos. If you feel stuck in patterns that are no longer serving you, I recommend CBT to help facilitate positive change and enhance coping strategies.

Remember that managing chaos is an ongoing process that evolves over time. While chaos never really disappears, our capacity to confront and cope with it can grow. It's okay to seek professional help if chaos significantly impacts your life and relationships. Therapists provide personalized guidance and support tailored to your needs, assisting you in achieving greater resilience and wellbeing.

PART TWO
ALL IS WELL

11

MOVING FROM CHAOS TO ALL IS WELL

I LOVE LIFE! I HAVE AN amazing wife who challenges, supports, and loves me. I have two cool children who inspire me. I have friends and family who make my life better. I've worked hard, and I now have the opportunity to travel and work around the world. I believe I'm living my best life. Yet, there is chaos.

Chaos is all around us. It's an undeniable part of life. Amid joy and success, we still encounter trauma, grief, anger, toxic people, and pain. Bad days and sadness are inevitable.

I've spent considerable time reconciling this paradox in my own life—how can I be in a good place while simultaneously facing life's challenges?

The key lies in actively striving to live our best lives and investing energy into things that foster personal growth and fulfillment. This approach allows us to better navigate the chaos and maintain a sense of equilibrium, finding solace in the notion that "All is well."

I like what the Dalai Lama said about the irony of human behavior, how people often sacrifice their health to earn money, then spend money to regain their health. They become so anxious about the future that they fail to enjoy the present, leading to a life in which they neither live in the moment nor in the future, ultimately never truly living. In other words, how are we really living? What exactly constitutes living our "best life?" Does it mean we blissfully go through life happily without challenges and chaos? I don't think so, and I doubt such a state is achievable without denying reality. Instead, it's about finding balance. Often, we don't recognize or experience true joy in our lives unless we've also experienced true chaos. Living our best lives does not necessarily happen because chaos is absent; rather, the two coexist.

Chaos serves as the catalyst in the mix of our lives, enhancing our experiences of joy, happiness, and the sense that *all is well*. Consider the yin and yang symbol—a fundamental concept in Chinese philosophy, illustrating the interconnectedness of opposing forces. Yin is negative and dark, and Yang is positive and bright. Their interplay is thought to maintain harmony in the universe and influence everything within it. One cannot occur without the other, highlighting the necessity of balance.

So, how can we reconcile the chaos and still find peace? How do we begin living our best lives with chaos all around? It's about acknowledging its presence and learning to coexist with it.

A sign on my office wall reads, "Engage the Chaos." This signifies embracing and navigating the chaos rather than attempting to evade or suppress it, which only perpetuates its hold on us.

Ultimately, the *all-is-well* mentality is not about achieving perfection or constant success. It's about acknowledging the chaos around us, making mindful choices, cultivating resilience, and practicing gratitude. It's about living authentically and with integrity.

The following sections will guide you through the complexities of chaos, empowering you to confront it while living your best life.

12

AWARENESS

AWARENESS IS CRUCIAL FOR NAVIGATING the chaos in our lives. It helps us manage both external and internal chaos by fostering a deeper understanding of ourselves, others, and our surroundings. Delving into our thoughts, emotions, and the present moment can be unsettling as it often reveals aspects of ourselves that we may not like. While awareness doesn't guarantee success or even happiness, I've found that embracing this mindset leads to better outcomes in our relationships, our work, and our overall lives. Our emotions, thoughts, and beliefs are an integral part of the human experience. By being aware of our emotions and acknowledging and accepting them, we can respond to the chaos in a more balanced way.

Emotional and cognitive awareness

Emotional awareness allows us to regulate our responses, manage stress, and maintain healthier relationships, which are crucial when facing chaos.

Cognitive awareness is less about our emotions and more about how we think. By recognizing our thought patterns, prejudices, and beliefs, we can develop a curious mindset. We can also challenge the beliefs and prejudices that limit us from developing, learning, and growing. By being cognitively aware, we can foster the innovation and creativity within ourselves.

Deconstructing our emotional and cognitive awareness is incredibly empowering. We all carry prejudices. Prejudice can be an insidious and powerful thing if it's unchecked. It can lead to racism, sexism, ageism, and other isms.

Growing up in Charlotte, NC, in the '70s, I had a front-row seat to the South in the post-civil rights movement era. Charlotte was where the busing case originated that went before the Supreme Court. There were race riots in high schools, and racial tensions were everywhere.

One response to this tension was to establish a club called Project Aires in middle and high schools throughout Charlotte. The club aimed to break down prejudices by promoting mutual understanding and respect among the races. Kids from different backgrounds would get together, talk, go on camps, dance, and laugh together. I still remember Teila and Norma, two African American classmates, trying to teach me how to dance in 7th grade. The result was fits of laughter from them and tearing up the dance floor to Michael Jackson from me! This is probably an overstatement, but hey, it's my story.

These experiences of engaging with one another, having conversations, and developing friendships did more to break down prejudices and combat racism than any school-based curriculum could ever do. Having real conversations and getting to know people of other ethnicities, cultures, and colors had a profoundly positive effect on how I see the world.

Even though my awareness was raised through this process, it would never be on par with the experiences my friends Teila and Norma faced as Black women growing up in the post-civil rights era South. Awareness does not automatically equate to understanding. It can help, but ultimately, I cannot change my experience as a White male growing up at the same time and place. I can try to understand, demonstrate empathy and kindness, and let my new awareness and limited understanding guide my actions and decisions.

By understanding ourselves and others, regulating our emotions, managing our thoughts, and staying present, we can approach chaos with greater confidence and resilience, leading to personal growth and successful outcomes.

One of my favorite books is *Awareness*, authored by Anthony de Mello, a Jesuit priest and spiritual teacher. De Mello's teachings blend Christian spirituality with Eastern philosophies, emphasizing the transformative power of awareness, mindfulness, and self-discovery on the path toward personal and spiritual growth.

De Mello covers a lot of ground in this book. He provides practical examples, mediations, and exercises to help us become more aware and mindful. The list here provides an overview of the book's central themes and teachings, which are aimed at helping individuals live more consciously and authentically:

❖ ACCEPTANCE AND FORGIVENESS: Encouraging readers to accept themselves and others as they are and to practice forgiveness.

- ❖ AWAKENING: Guiding readers toward a state of awakening, where they see the world more clearly, experience inner peace, and live in harmony with themselves and others.

- ❖ FREEDOM FROM JUDGMENT: Encouraging readers to suspend judgment and observe without attaching labels or interpretations to their experiences.

- ❖ EMBRACING CHANGE: Encouraging readers to embrace change and the impermanence of life as a source of growth and transformation. Top of Form

A word of warning, though: de Mello makes it clear that being "awake" can be filled with peril. If you're awake and aware and others are not, it can cause strife. If you choose to take the journey toward awareness, remember that some people in your life may choose to go through life asleep. Being awake can be difficult, and once you are awake and aware of all that is happening around you, you can't go back to being unaware or asleep.

The following are different aspects of awareness that are worth exploring in our own lives:

Own your own shit – self-awareness

Another great thing I used to hear from my mother growing up was, "Own your own shit," meaning that if we screw up, we should own it. Of course, we should also claim it if we do something well. Owning your own shit is about self-awareness, which is one of the foundations of personal growth and development. It involves understanding our strengths, weaknesses, values, beliefs, and motivations.

Self-awareness enables us to make conscious choices, set goals, and make decisions that align with our authentic selves. By knowing who we are and what we want, we can navigate challenges with clarity and purpose. I continually work on being in a place where I can recognize and address it. If I screw up and it involves other people, I try to own my part of it. It often requires an apology or conversation on my part. Sometimes, it doesn't work, but my responsibility is to try to make things right.

During my son's last couple of years in high school, whenever he got in trouble at school or didn't do well, he would blame his teachers. Blaming others became a habit. I started challenging him about it, asking questions like, "What did the teacher do?" "What did you do/not do?" "Who is responsible for your behavior?" and "Who is responsible for the results of your test?" Nine times out of ten, he would reflect and change his tune. He would own his behavior, whether acting out in class or not studying for a test. Sometimes, we need others to help us move toward self-awareness by holding up the mirror and providing feedback or an alternative perspective.

The shadow

One of the aspects of self-awareness that fascinates me is the role of our shadow self. Carl Jung, the Swiss psychologist, spoke a lot about the shadow. According to Jung, the shadow refers to our personality's unconscious and repressed aspects. It encompasses all the qualities, desires, impulses, and emotions we deny or reject within ourselves, often considering them to be negative, undesirable, or socially unacceptable.

I like to think of the shadow as the parts of ourselves we may not like or want to acknowledge, yet they influence our actions, decisions, and interactions with others. Acknowledging and exploring these aspects of ourselves can be scary, but without our shadow, we don't have a reflection of the good and positive things in ourselves.

Unfortunately, many of us are trained and socialized from birth not to show weakness. We're told that the things we don't like about ourselves, the negative, should be hidden. So, we bury our shadow deep within.

The challenge is that when we're experiencing chaos, our shadow can bubble up. It can emerge in its full glory, and we, and those around us, are caught off guard. We may not be equipped to recognize and deal with those aspects of ourselves that we have deeply buried.

It's important to remember that the shadow is part of us, and although it doesn't define us, we need to be aware of it. Understanding and knowing our shadow self is an important part of developing into our best self. Often, these are things that we only see or know about ourselves, but sometimes, they are things that others see, and we don't.

The opportunity is for us to do some work now, so that we can begin to recognize the different aspects of our personalities and lives. Acknowledging and addressing the shadow in ourselves is critical to our self-development, growth, and move into the *all is well*.

Opportunities awareness provides for living our best lives

Awareness plays a crucial role in living a fulfilling and successful life. Being conscious and mindful of one's thoughts, emotions, and surroundings has several significant implications:

❖ HEALTH AND WELLBEING: Awareness of one's physical health and the need for exercise, nutrition, and sleep is crucial for a healthy lifestyle. Being mindful of your body's needs can lead to a longer, stronger, and more enjoyable life.

❖ PERSONAL RELATIONSHIPS: Awareness of your emotions and the emotions of others is vital for building and maintaining healthy relationships. It enables effective communication, empathy, and conflict resolution.

❖ PERSONAL GROWTH: Self-awareness is a cornerstone of personal development. Understanding your strengths and weaknesses allows you to set goals, make improvements, and live a more fulfilling life.

❖ RESILIENCE: Awareness of your own mental and emotional state is essential for building resilience. When you're aware of your coping mechanisms and emotional responses, you can bounce back from adversity more effectively.

❖ PURPOSE AND MEANING: Reflecting on your values and what gives your life purpose is a form of awareness. It can lead to a more meaningful and fulfilling existence.

❖ MINDFULNESS: Practicing mindfulness allows us to be fully aware of the present moment without judgment. It can reduce stress, increase happiness, and improve overall wellbeing.

Cultivating awareness through meditation, journaling, and self-reflection can be transformative. These things help us make better decisions, understand ourselves and others better, and navigate the complexities of an ever-changing world more effectively.

Story: The Stonecutter

Years ago, I worked with an amazing guy named Lance in North Carolina who was a great storyteller. One story Lance told was about a stonecutter. Here's what I remember.

Once there was a stonecutter. He worked hard every day, cutting stone from a mountain to carve into useful and beautiful items to sell. However, he was tired of cutting and carving stone. He wanted something more. He wished he could be rich and powerful.

The next day, the King ordered a large stone be carved into a bird. The stonecutter worked hard for weeks. When he finally finished it, he delivered the stone carving to the King. The King was so impressed that he immediately made the stonecutter a duke and gave him land, wealth, and a castle to live in. The stonecutter couldn't believe his luck. He was rich and powerful.

One day, the stonecutter, now a duke, was riding his horse when he noticed that the Sun was shining on him and he could feel himself getting sunburnt. He thought, *I am a duke. I'm rich and powerful, but the Sun is more powerful. It is hot and bright. I wish I were the Sun.*

Instantly, he became the Sun. He shone brightly on the Earth. *I am the most powerful now*, he thought. *I'm the Sun!* Just then, a cloud passed before him, and the sky grew dark. *That cloud is more powerful than the Sun*, he thought. *I wish I were a cloud.*

Instantly, he became a cloud. He moved across the sky to sunny places and covered the Sun. Just then, a big wind came and blew the clouds away, and the Sun came back out. *The wind is more powerful than the cloud*, he thought. *I wish I were the wind.*

Instantly, he became the wind. He blew clouds across the sky and blew trees, their branches swaying this way and that. Just then, he came upon a mountain and tried to blow it out of his way. However, the mountain did not move. *The mountain is more powerful than the wind*, he thought. *I wish I were a mountain.*

Instantly, he became a mountain. He stood tall and proud. No wind, clouds, or Sun affected him. However, one day, he felt a piece of himself being chipped off and noticed a little man, a stonecutter, cutting away at him. *The stonecutter is more powerful than a mountain*, he thought. *I wish I were a stonecutter.*

Instantly, he became a stonecutter again, and he was content.

This story illustrates the stonecutter's journey of self-awareness. As he desires to become more powerful, he gains insight into his place in the universe. Ultimately, the stonecutter's realization comes not from gaining more wealth or power but from recognizing the value of his own existence. Awareness is about seeking insight and understanding about ourselves and others. By doing so, we, like the stonecutter, can figure out where we fit into this hectic world.

LIFE HACKS

Becoming more aware can be a life-changing experience, but it also takes work. Here are a few life hacks for practicing awareness:

Mindfulness
Meditation and Breathing Exercises

As previously discussed, meditation is proven to help with mindfulness and being centered, which leads to greater awareness. I came late to meditation, but it is now an important part of my daily routine. If you need a place to start, I suggest trying Metta meditation—also known as loving-kindness meditation.

I also practice different breathing techniques. Box breathing is a great one. Breathe in for 3-5 seconds, hold for 3-5 seconds, exhale for 3-5 seconds, hold for 3-5 seconds, then repeat. While doing box breathing, I think about where I am and what I'm grateful for and try to be present, letting the thoughts come and go without trying to control them.

JOURNALING
KEEP A DAILY JOURNAL
Journaling each day can help you better understand your emotions and encourage regular reflection. At the end of every day, try to write down any memorable events, and the things you're grateful for. You could start by answering some of the following questions:

❖ What was meaningful about my day?

❖ What were the best and worst moments of my day?

❖ What were my dominant emotions?

❖ What did I learn about myself?

❖ How did I treat others?

❖ What am I grateful for?

❖ What could I have done better?

It can also be helpful to read your old journal entries occasionally to see how you've changed and developed.

ACTIONS

SEEK FEEDBACK FROM OTHERS

Find a trusted friend or family member and ask them to give you some honest feedback. You can tell them that you're trying to develop greater self-awareness and that you'd appreciate honest answers to your questions—not answers that make you feel better. You can ask questions like:

- ❖ What's my greatest strength?

- ❖ What's something I could improve on?

- ❖ What dynamic do I bring to a social situation?

- ❖ Am I someone you would go to for either advice or comfort?

- ❖ When am I at my best?

- ❖ What do you think my values are in my relationships and at work?

- ❖ Do I have strengths in one context that may be a weakness in another—and vice versa?

13

GRATITUDE

ONE OF THE SYMPTOMS OF a chaotic society is the lack of gratitude. We get so caught up in our own needs, wants, emotions, problems, and stress that we do not pause and consider all that we have to be thankful for. It seems, as a society, we feel increasingly entitled to receive good things in our lives, and when they happen, instead of being grateful, we shrug and say to ourselves that we deserve them. This attitude misses the whole point of gratitude.

After a traumatic event a few years ago, I was a wreck. I couldn't sleep, I was not coping, and I was drinking more than I should. I felt like I was in a chaos storm that I could not escape. I was in a repeating loop of fear, anxiety, and anger.

My wife could see the turmoil I was in and challenged me to shift my focus from all that was difficult and out of my control to all the good things that surrounded us and what I could control. Although it was difficult to switch as we were both struggling, the truth was we were in a beautiful part of the world, meeting good people, making new friends, and we had each other. I remember one day, we packed a picnic, went down to the ocean, and watched the sunset. It was breathtakingly beautiful, and we experienced it for free. Even though I was anxious and afraid, by pausing, taking some deep breaths, and focusing on the present goodness around me, I was overcome with gratitude and calm, and the anxiety subsided.

Gratitude is a powerful and positive emotional response that involves recognizing and appreciating the goodness in our lives. It's the feeling of thankfulness for the experiences, people, and things that bring us positivity and value. Gratitude goes beyond just saying thank you; it involves genuinely acknowledging the blessings and positive aspects of our lives, even when we're in chaos. It's not a quid pro quo concept in which we are thankful in the hopes of gaining or receiving more. It just is. Either we are grateful, or we are not. When living in the *all is well*, gratitude also means demonstrating kindness to others. We are paying it forward.

Gratitude is the ability to experience life as a gift. It requires intention. Each day, I take time to think for a moment about what I'm grateful for. Often, this is a part of my morning or evening routine. I like to show appreciation for where I am, what I have, and who I love. When I do this and demonstrate it in my actions, I've seen how it can transform my mindset. It's another superpower of the *all is well*.

Out of all the tools in our human arsenal, gratitude is the most powerful. I like the research showing how experiences result in greater long-term happiness than material possessions. In our instant gratification and 24/7 online shopping world, it's interesting that the happiness derived from things slowly diminishes while the happiness associated with experiences increases over time. Experiences become more memorable and important because they're often shared with others. I want to fill my life with more experiences shared with the people I love rather than the accumulation of more material possessions.

Story: Surgery Without Walls

In high school, I had the opportunity to travel to the Dominican Republic for two summers on medical mission trips. A team of doctors and volunteers would fly to the DR for a week or two and set up medical clinics in churches throughout the countryside. Most people we saw were Haitian migrant workers who came across the border yearly to harvest the sugar cane. They worked for 50 cents per day. The diseases the doctors saw and treated were often ones they'd only ever read about in their textbooks in medical school. The people we connected with were some of the poorest in the world. They had few material possessions and had a low life expectancy. Looking from the outside, you could see the hopelessness of their situation.

However, as I reflect on those trips now, the thing that stands out is the gratitude of the people we served. Not only the gratitude for us being there and providing much-needed medicine and medical care, but their gratitude for each other and for life itself. Specifically, I remember people standing in long lines for hours in the hot sun waiting for a doctor to see them. They never complained, always smiled, and were so thankful to all of us.

I remember one hot day when a woman brought her very sick son to the clinic. After examining him, the doctors determined that he had acute appendicitis. They quickly decided that the boy, Martine, was critical and needed surgery. Fortunately, our team included a surgeon who had spent years working in a leper colony in India and was experienced in performing surgery under primitive conditions. He and a nurse swiftly set up a makeshift operating theater with sheets for walls and prepared for the procedure. A surgical kit and some ether were found, and the nurse quickly assumed the role of anesthesiologist, carefully administering ether as the doctor performed the appendectomy.

I had the opportunity to witness the entire process. However, what has stayed with me all these years is not the heroics of the medical team who saved Martine's life but the response of his mother. A week later, we were running a clinic in a nearby village. Martine's mother arrived towards the end of the day and insisted we come to her house for dinner.

Her home had wooden walls, a dirt floor, and a roof made of banana leaves. Since we could not all fit inside, we sat around makeshift tables outside her home. The meal she prepared was amazing: plantains, yuca, beans, rice, and beef. It was a feast filled with laughter, fellowship, and celebration. We celebrated life. I was deeply moved by the fact that she had so little yet organized this meal to thank us for saving her son's life.

Opportunities gratitude provides for living our best lives

Gratitude can improve our wellbeing by reducing stress and increasing satisfaction. One of the great things about gratitude is that it shifts the focus from what we don't have to what we do have, which brings us into the present. This change in mindset can be helpful as we navigate chaos. Have you ever noticed how stress and anxiety increase when we focus on the negative? Alternatively, gratitude can build our emotional resilience by grounding us and switching our focus to what we have right here, right now. It helps us bounce back faster and keep us moving forward.

Gratitude can also be a powerful positive force in our interpersonal relationships. Here are some examples:

❖ ENHANCED EMPATHY: By practicing gratitude, we encourage empathy by better understanding and appreciating the efforts, kindness, and contributions of others.

❖ STRONGER CONNECTIONS: By expressing our gratitude to and for others, we build positivity. When people feel appreciated, they're more likely to continue being supportive.

❖ BETTER OUTCOMES: Gratitude can help improve outcomes, particularly during conflict. By reminding ourselves of the positive aspects of the other person and our relationship with them, it allows us to approach disagreements with more understanding and a cooperative attitude.

❖ INCREASED GENEROSITY: When we experience gratitude, we're more likely to pay it forward and be kind and generous toward others.

LIFE HACKS

JOURNALING

Here is a good way to do some gratitude journaling—simply reflect on and list the things you're grateful for. This can help you appreciate all the good things that surround you. Some of the following prompts may help to get you started:

❖ What's one thing that made me smile today?

- ❖ Who are two people in my life I'm thankful for?
- ❖ What activity or hobby brought me joy in the past week?
- ❖ What's my favorite thing about being in the outdoors?
- ❖ What's one act of kindness I experienced or witnessed in the past week?
- ❖ What are three things about my current life that I'm thankful for?

ACTIONS

My favorite hack for increasing my gratitude is using guided questions to talk with someone I trust. For example, a few questions I use are:

- ❖ What am I grateful for?
- ❖ What am I proud of?
- ❖ What would I like to keep doing, stop doing or start doing?
- ❖ What am I looking forward to?

Pausing to reflect on the things I'm grateful for is a powerful exercise that brings more joy and abundance into my life.

14

RESILIENCY

HAVE YOU EVER NOTICED THAT sometimes when chaos hits, our ability to respond is lower than we would like it to be? Sometimes, I feel like I'm going backward in responding to and dealing with the chaos. I'm like a deer caught in the headlights. I see and feel the chaos, but I feel powerless to act. It's at these times when I remember that I am resilient. I think of all the times I've faced horrible things or dealt with difficult people or situations and how I coped and overcame them with my integrity intact. I was okay.

Resiliency is an amazing thing. In many ways, it is our superpower against chaos. Resiliency is the ability to bounce back, adapt, cope, and recover from adversity. It encompasses mental, emotional, physical, and social aspects of our lives and plays a crucial role in personal wellbeing and professional success. The great thing about resiliency is that it can be learned. By developing and strengthening our resiliency, we can better face whatever chaos throws our way.

Most of us have a personal story of resilience, something we, a family member or friend, have overcome—surviving cancer, abuse, loss, addiction, or a breakdown in a relationship or business.

Before writing this book, I faced a massive test of my resiliency. A business I was in ended suddenly. I realized I was dealing with toxic people. I was lost. I felt grief, anger, and sadness. I began to question my own abilities, knowledge, and strengths. I had invested a year and a half of my life in the project and the people I was working with. There was no discussion or communication. There was no opportunity to address concerns, fix problems, or move forward in any way. It was over. I was in chaos.

So, how did I get out of it? I relied on my resiliency. Resiliency is a mindset that says I will bounce back. I will make it! I have dealt with tough stuff before, and I can do it again. I began focusing on what was important to me—my family and friends, my community, and my mental and physical health. I focused on the present, not what had happened or may happen in the future. My friends and family supported me, listened, and challenged me to take action and take control. At times, I had to speak to myself like I spoke to my children when they were toddlers. I had to let myself know that everything would be okay and that I was in control, not the situation or those idiots I'd been working with. I was in charge of myself, my decisions, and my abilities and gifts. This didn't mean I felt any less pain. It didn't mean I grieved any less. It meant that I could begin to focus on moving on. I disciplined myself to exercise, eat well, do breathwork, and appreciate all the small things like watching sunsets, walking in nature, and listening to music.

Resiliency doesn't mean ignoring it, and it will go away. It means you work through the stuff, and you realize you can and will bounce back. I also believe that when we bounce back we're stronger and more aware.

Recently, my wife and I were playing the card game *Vertellis* (meaning tell us more in Dutch). Round one consists of thought-provoking questions. One of the cards asked, "What were the best and worst things that happened in the past year?" When I thought about it, I realized it was the same thing. The breakdown in the business was easily the worst thing, but on reflection, it was also the best thing that happened. Yes, it was a difficult experience, but I had come through it—not just surviving but now thriving. I was stronger than I thought, learned a lot about myself, met good people, and realized how much I had to be grateful for.

Story: Couch Surfing Through Senior Year

I had a good friend named Jimmy in high school. Jimmy was super smart, funny, and a nice guy. He had always suffered from chronic asthma and other health problems. His mother and father had been abusive but had now left the scene. No one knew where they were. Jimmy had been in and out of foster homes where he had experienced more abuse.

I'm not sure how Jimmy had the tenacity to keep going. One of the things I remember most is that he always had a smile on his face. He never complained.

By the time Jimmy started his junior year in high school, he was homeless. He'd told the authorities he was living with an older sister to avoid the foster care system. He began to couch surf at friends' houses, including mine. However, most of the time, he stayed with our friend Mark. Mark's mom was amazing. She was a single parent raising three kids, and Jimmy fit right in.

Jimmy got a job working at a gas station that sold beer on the county line, so he worked most nights till 1:00 AM. With his late nights, health issues, and lack of consistent housing, Jimmy was often absent from school. In fact, by the final week of our senior year, Jimmy had been absent 29 days that year. If he missed one more day, he would have had to repeat his senior year. He made it, graduating with a strong A/B average and getting a scholarship to college.

Jimmy now runs a successful business and has a wonderful family. I caught up with Jimmy a couple of years ago. We went out, had a few beers, and reminisced about the good ole days. I asked him how he survived those last two years of high school. He said, "I figured that this was the situation I was in, and I could either sink or swim. The choice was mine. Also, I didn't do it on my own. I had help. Mark's mom and others took me in and cared for me."

This only increased my admiration for Jimmy. He not only survived in horrible circumstances, but he also thrived. He chose to take responsibility for his situation even though he didn't cause it. He kept bouncing back. Jimmy didn't sit around feeling sorry for himself. Resiliency can only grow and be fostered when there is action taken to do something about the chaos rather than letting it consume you. Wishing it to stop or blaming others won't fix anything.

Cultivating resiliency involves developing coping strategies, such as building a strong support network, practicing stress management techniques, looking after your physical and mental health and maintaining a positive outlook on life.

Opportunities resiliency provides for living our best lives

Developing resiliency can greatly impact our mental health and ability to thrive in a chaotic world. Here are some of the benefits of developing resiliency in our lives:

- ❖ ADAPTATION TO CHANGE: When going through grief or significant change, we go through different stages. Resiliency helps us adapt to this cycle of change and move toward acceptance. In a chaotic world, the ability to navigate these changes is invaluable.

- ❖ COPING WITH STRESS: Resilient individuals are better equipped to manage stress. It can help us handle high-pressure situations, remain composed, and make rational decisions even when faced with adversity.

- ❖ EMOTIONAL STRENGTH: Resiliency is closely tied to emotional wellbeing. It allows us to acknowledge and process our emotions healthily rather than being overwhelmed by them. This emotional strength helps us maintain mental health and an overall sense of wellbeing.

- ❖ RELATIONSHIPS: Resiliency helps us foster positive interpersonal relationships. When we are emotionally resilient, we're often better at communicating, empathizing, and maintaining healthy connections, both in personal and professional settings.

LIFE HACKS

<u>MINDFULNESS</u>

❖ LEARN FROM EXPERIENCE: You may have heard the saying that experience is the best teacher. This is so true. However, we must first be prepared to learn from our experiences. We can think about previous times of chaos in our lives and consider the skills and strategies that helped us through those difficult times. I find writing about traumatic experiences in a journal or talking them through with a friend helps me identify positive and negative behavior patterns—and guides my future behavior.

❖ REMAIN HOPEFUL: When we're in chaos, we can lose hope. To build resiliency, we can reflect on the things for which we are grateful. At the same time, we must realize that the past is the past. We cannot change it. Instead, we can look forward to the future. It will be different. It can be better. Accepting and anticipating change makes it easier to adapt and view new challenges with less anxiety, and perhaps as an opportunity.

<u>ACTIONS</u>

❖ GET INVOLVED, GET CONNECTED: Building strong, positive relationships with friends and loved ones can provide you with needed support, guidance, and acceptance in good and bad times. Get connected with your local community. A great way to get connected is through volunteering. I have a friend who volunteers twice a week at a charity helping the homeless. She says it's the best part of her week. Maybe you could join an art class, take dance lessons, or enroll in a personal or professional development course. You could also consider joining a faith or spiritual community. These are all great ways to make new connections and share common experiences. When we do things like this, it fosters resiliency in our lives.

❖ MAKE EVERY DAY MEANINGFUL: When we make the most of each day, it tends to have a flow-on effect for the rest of our lives. Start small by setting clear, achievable goals every day. Do something that gives you a sense of accomplishment and purpose each day. Each night, my wife and I discuss our plans and goals for the next day. By stating our goals, we can support and hold each other accountable for reaching them.

❖ TAKE CARE AND BE WELL: Addressing our own needs and feelings is important for being resilient. Finding opportunities to participate in activities and hobbies that we enjoy is useful and builds strength. This can include physical activity in our daily routine. Getting plenty of sleep and creating consistent bedtime rituals is also critical. This is a hard one for me, but I'm working on it! Eating a healthy diet and practicing stress management and relaxation techniques, such as yoga, meditation, guided imagery, deep breathing, or prayer, are also resilience-building activities.

❖ BE PROACTIVE: I still sometimes ignore the problems and challenges that chaos brings, hoping they will go away. But they never do. We can build resiliency by being proactive and not ignoring challenging situations—figuring out what needs to be done, making a plan, and taking action.

15

CHOICES

IN MY FRESHMAN YEAR OF college, I had a religion professor who assigned two texts for our Old Testament class. Of course, the Bible was the first text, and the second was *East of Eden* by John Steinbeck. From that day, John Steinbeck became one of my favorite authors. In *East of Eden*, there's a central theme or concept called Timshel. It's a Hebrew word that means "thou mayest," and it's all about the power of choice. The book reminds us that we can shape our own paths, that we're not just stuck following some predestined script.

It's a strong and incredibly empowering theme. The characters in the story struggle with their inner demons, face tough moral decisions, and deal with the consequences of their actions. Through it all, Timshel is this constant reminder that we have choices and that our choices matter. Our choices have real weight and can completely change our lives. It's a call to action, to recognize the impact our decisions can have on ourselves and those around us. Timshel gives us hope, urging us to seek personal growth, redemption, and a life that truly means something.

So, how does this apply to when we're in chaos? Do choices really matter? How can these choices help us move into the *all is well*? Do choices increase or decrease our power?

I remember reading Stephen Covey's *7 Habits of Highly Successful People* in the early 1990s. I still refer to it when working with executives and companies. One of the sections that resonated with me was the one on being proactive or reactive and the proactive choices we can make when things aren't going well.

Over the years, I've explored how the power dynamic of personal or positional power affects our roles and relationships. The power dynamic refers to how authority, influence, and control are distributed and used within a relationship, group, organization, and even society. It defines how individuals or entities interact with one another based on their relative positions of power.

Power can be formal and informal, stemming from various sources such as position, expertise, charisma, resources, and/or social connections. Power dynamics play a significant role in shaping interactions and outcomes in both work and personal life. Understanding and navigating power dynamics can lead to positive results and healthier relationships. Working with people and organizations over the years, I've seen how power is wielded with both positive and negative results.

As leaders or in our personal lives, recognizing power dynamics can—pardon the pun—be empowering. It allows us to see how much power we have to affect change, improve situations, and obtain results. Many times, this power may be limited. However, by putting our time, energy, and focus into our powerful choices, circumstances can transform, and our power grows. Exercising powerful choices increases the likelihood of improving our position, resources, expertise, connections, or network, thereby increasing our power.

Still, a new model based on our understanding of power dynamics is called for. We do have choices in chaos. To understand our powerful choices, we first have to think about how we currently respond to crises. Are the choices we make in response to chaos powerful or powerless?

Powerful choices

Powerful means full of power, and these choices increase our power, influence, and opportunity. To be effective in chaos, we should consciously try to work through these choices as often as possible. If we're not exercising these powerful choices, and instead pour our energy into how people behave or make us feel, then by default, we give what little power we have away and miss an opportunity to grow it and successfully navigate power dynamics.

These are the four powerful choices we have when experiencing chaos:

- ❖ Focus;
- ❖ Accept it;
- ❖ Work it;
- ❖ Leave.

Focus: Many people in the midst of chaos feel disempowered. The focus choice requires us to stop and try to understand what power we have in a situation. Focusing on the power we do have is critical to making powerful choices. This may sound redundant, but it's true. A good set of questions to consider is, "How much power do I have to change or influence this situation?" and "Where is that power or influence located?"

ACCEPT IT: This choice is about living with the current situation. Maybe it's not worth fighting or changing. Perhaps we don't have enough power to do anything about it. So, the question is, "Can I live with it?" If so, great, move on. If not, then you either need to work on the problem or leave.

WORK IT: Working on the problem is all about trying to fix or improve your situation. You have focused and realized your power, and you can't just accept it, so work on it. Do what you can in your area of power or influence to make changes, influence others, and build your power. Ask yourself what solutions you can provide. Remember to keep the solutions focused on the actual problem.

LEAVE: This choice comes into play when you've focused on your power, you've chosen not to accept the chaos, you've tried to work it out, and you're still not getting an outcome that works. The chaos is still there, draining or destroying you. Therefore, the final powerful choice is to leave. Maybe that's leaving a job or a relationship or just letting go and turning your back on that situation to focus on something else.

So, how does this all work in real life? One of the best stories I know about exercising powerful choices involves my brother Dan.

Story: The Teacher Is The Student

When Dan graduated from college, he went to work as a biology teacher for a high school in Western NC. He was excited, energized, and ready to go. He had a solid educational and theoretical background and knew his subject matter. By Christmas break, though, things had changed. Dan was struggling with the chaos of his new job and complaining a lot.

As the Christmas break went on, so did Dan. He spent a lot of time asking us rhetorical questions and informing us of how difficult it was. He was in chaos and was trying to figure it out. The litany of responses to the chaos went something like this:

"Man, this sucks.

I have apathetic students who don't study.

Parents don't show up at parent-teacher conferences.

When I ask other teachers if they want to collaborate, they laugh and walk away.

Our budget keeps getting cut, and we don't have resources for the classroom.

The bureaucracy is crazy. Just to take kids on a field trip, you must get permission from the principal, send home permission slips for parents to sign, reserve a bus driver, and submit a budget.

The state Department of Public Instruction has changed our curriculum requirements twice in three months!"

After a while, we got tired of hearing about Dan's troubles, and my older brother asked him, "Hey, man, where's your power?"

Dan thought about this question and realized what little power he had was in his classroom. Then, he got busy.

Over the remaining Christmas break, he rewrote his curriculum to focus on environmental science. When school started, he met with the principal and got approval to change his curriculum. He started taking his kids on field trips into Pisgah National Forest—a few miles from the school—and they started doing water testing on local waterways.

Dan put in a request to the school for $700 for hip waders, nets, and other tools so his kids could start collecting samples. The principal was so impressed that he had a teacher who was "working on it" that he approved the request.

The agriculture science teacher noticed his passion and approached him with a proposition to combine their classes. They would take both classes to farms to conduct soil and water tests, sharing the data and results. One benefit of this partnership was that students from both classes began to see the value in each other's subjects. Soon, students from other classes also took notice, and agricultural and environmental science became the two most popular electives in the school.

Then, Dan got his bus driver's license so he wouldn't have to reserve one whenever he wanted to take the kids into the field.

In the teacher's lounge, he started getting grilled by some of the old guard teachers. "How did you get all that money from the school?"

"I asked for it," was Dan's reply.

"Well, how do you get permission to go on all those field trips?"

"I don't ask. My curriculum has been approved... My classroom, my rules," Dan said.

Before the next parent-teacher conference, Dan sent a letter home with each student, saying that if a parent didn't show up or set up a call for a parent-teacher conference, he would mark down all students by one grade.

Dan said he walked into the classroom the night of the parent-teacher conference to about 35 angry parents. He calmed them down, apologized for the ruse, and said, "Now let's talk about your kids, what we're doing in the classroom, and what they need from you." Parents then began volunteering and helping out.

After his first year teaching, Dan was named Teacher of the Year for the high school. After his second year, he was named one of the most creative teachers of the year for the state!

So, what changed? The bureaucracy was still there. Budget constraints were still a reality. Many other teachers still didn't want to collaborate. Well, Dan focused his energy on a different place. He moved from powerless choices, where he was giving away his power, to powerful choices, where his power, influence, and opportunities increased. He focused on the problem and realized where his power was and how much power he had.

Dan couldn't live with it, so he decided to act. He worked on the problems based on his power. Eventually, Dan left teaching; he burned out. However, when he chose to leave, it was still a powerful choice, and he left on his own terms.

The amazing thing about powerful choices is that when you use them your power will increase. However, if you focus on the chaos and things outside of your control then your power will decrease. I know this may sound simplistic but it's true.

Powerful Choices

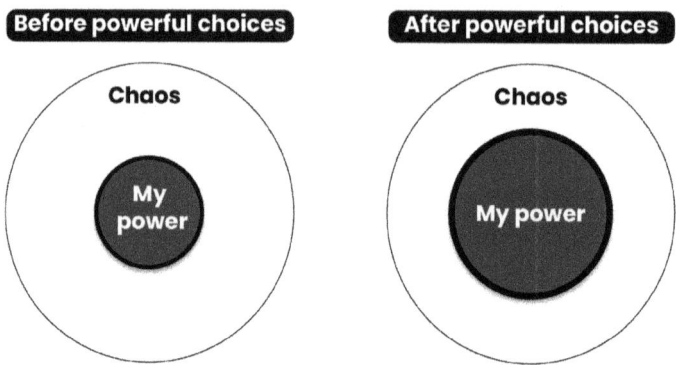

Opportunities powerful choices provide for living our best lives

I try to practice my powerful choices daily. Sometimes, when I'm in chaos, and there's pain, trauma, fear, or anger, it's difficult. This is when I need to practice my choices the most. If I give in to the fear, anger, and trauma, then my power diminishes, and I shrink. I always try to remain conscious of my choices; I surround myself with trustworthy people who have my back. They often act as sounding boards, listen, and ask questions. This gives me perspective and allows me to explore my powerful choices more objectively.

LIFE HACKS

ACTIONS

Practicing powerful choices has massive implications. When you're next in chaos, try it.

1. Choose a problem or challenge you're currently experiencing.
2. Focus on where your power is and how much power you have to change or influence the situation.
3. Review your power choices.
4. If you can accept it, then do so and move on.
5. If you can't accept it, then try to work on the problem.
6. Document this process and track your progress. Is it working? Are you gaining power in the situation? If so, keep going. If not, explore your final choice, which is to leave.
7. Remember, a good outcome is one in which you keep your integrity intact.

16
AUTHENTICITY

AUTHENTICITY MEANS DIFFERENT THINGS TO different people. Often, when working with an executive team, I'll ask what authenticity means to them. Usually, I get some variation on the following: honesty, walking the talk, following through, values, morals, moral compass, and being congruent and ethical. These are all great words to describe authenticity. Authenticity is a fundamental moral and ethical principle that refers to honesty, truthfulness, and maintaining strong moral principles and values. It means consistency between our words, actions, and beliefs. When we act authentically, we adhere to a strong internal compass that guides our decisions and behavior, even when faced with chaos.

In the context of leadership, authenticity is paramount. An authentic leader is someone who leads by example, earning the trust and respect of their followers. My friend Denis describes this as leading from the front—in other words, someone who is in the trenches with you. These leaders demonstrate honesty, transparency, and accountability, creating an environment of openness and trust within their team or organization. Authentic leaders inspire subordinates to follow suit and foster a culture of ethics and high standards.

Story: In The Kitchen With Janet

When I was 15, I got my first job washing dishes in a summer camp kitchen. I had attended the camp as a child and was excited to finally join the staff. I'd arrived a couple of days before camp started to help clean and prepare the kitchen. My boss was a woman named Janet. She was in charge of food service and the kitchen at the camp. She was an amazing cook and managed a staff of about twenty; some were teenagers washing dishes like me, and others were KPs and cooks. She told me and two others to meet her at the kitchen at 7:30 PM on the first day to do a deep clean of the kitchen.

We arrived and began cleaning. Janet didn't just provide cleaning supplies, tell us what to do, and leave, she started cleaning along with us—pointing out things, encouraging us, and working circles around us. At 11:00 PM, the two others made an excuse and left. We were all exhausted, but Janet looked at me and asked if I wanted to keep going. "Yes," I said. Together, we worked until 2:00 AM, even scrubbing the grout between the tiles with toothbrushes. At the end of the night, Janet thanked me and said the kitchen had never looked better. I was proud but tired. I went to bed and was back in the kitchen at 7:00 AM for breakfast service.

After that, I returned every summer to work for Janet in the kitchen in different roles. I worked for her for many years. After college, I took a job as an assistant director at the camp. One of my duties was to run the food service, kitchen, etc. By then, Janet had left the camp but consulted with me and gave me valuable training and advice. Janet has become a close friend, and I have incredible admiration for her personally and professionally.

That first night we worked together is seared into my memory. I often look back and think about that night, sitting on my hands and knees scrubbing the floor. Janet was the best boss I ever had and, by far, one of the most authentic people I've ever met. Not just because she was a hard worker but because she also walked the talk. She never asked others to do something she wouldn't do. She listened and carefully considered others' opinions, challenged others, and gave feedback, often holding up a mirror to others' behaviors. She gave us room to succeed or fail on our own. Janet would say about managing others, "I give people a long rope; they can swing from it or hang themselves, but if they can't hold on, I'll be there to catch them." She also constantly looks for ways to improve herself, learn, and develop.

Saying you act with authenticity is one thing, but actually doing it can be hard and is a lifelong journey. How many times do we see people in leadership, whether they be politicians, corporate leaders, or professionals, talk about integrity or being authentic? They say it, yet their actions reflect an opposite reality. Their actions speak louder than their words. In fact, their actions are screaming. This may be because they haven't done the work necessary to integrate what they say and do. However, I get it. Integration or acting authentically—being honest, holding up the mirror, and living your values—can be perilous.

I'm sometimes asked, "What if someone claims to be authentic but acts unkindly, disrespectfully, or even cruelly?" Here's my take: saying the right words isn't enough. Authenticity doesn't sow division, fear, or hurt. It's about consistency and congruency. It's about saying and doing the right thing. Look closely—where there's authenticity, there's healing and positive actions. Anything else is just not the real deal.

Here's the thing about living and leading with authenticity—it's a journey of inner work before it becomes an outer practice with your friends, loved ones, colleagues or team. It demands your time, energy and a whole lot of intention.

However, here's the kicker: it's also a journey that forces us to face parts of ourselves that we may not want to see. That shadow we talked about earlier tends to rear its head. We may find ourselves wrestling with it rather than embracing it.

In my journey to live and act with authenticity, I've had some breakthrough moments in which everything just clicks. It feels good, like I'm in perfect harmony. However, there are also those times when I stumble. Broken promises, hurt feelings, and me feeling like shit—they are all part of the journey. Still, despite the messiness, this journey can be incredibly freeing and fulfilling.

So, how do we live a life of authenticity? For starters, we need to recognize that it's a journey. We may never arrive, or when we do, we may not recognize ourselves.

The previously explored concepts are the backbone of living and leading authentically. Think of them as the groundwork—the essential prep work we must do before fully embracing a life of authenticity. This groundwork propels us into the place where *all is well*. It's about navigating the chaos and understanding how fear, anger, and past traumas can throw us off course. However, once we're aware of these influences, we can avoid becoming the kind of people who dish out fear, anger, and trauma—whether it's in our personal relationships or the workplace. It's about breaking free from those toxic cycles and exercising your powerful choices.

Authentic Life Model

Years ago, my brother and I developed a model around living and leading with integrity, which today I refer to as the Authentic Life Model. I use this model with leaders and in my personal life to live into the *all is well*. In my experience, classic self-development-informed approaches focus on improving skills or knowledge, whereas spiritually-informed approaches focus on something more esoteric. This model combines the two: supporting and challenging, focusing on skills and techniques, and letting go to focus on a more spiritual side.

Authentic Life Model

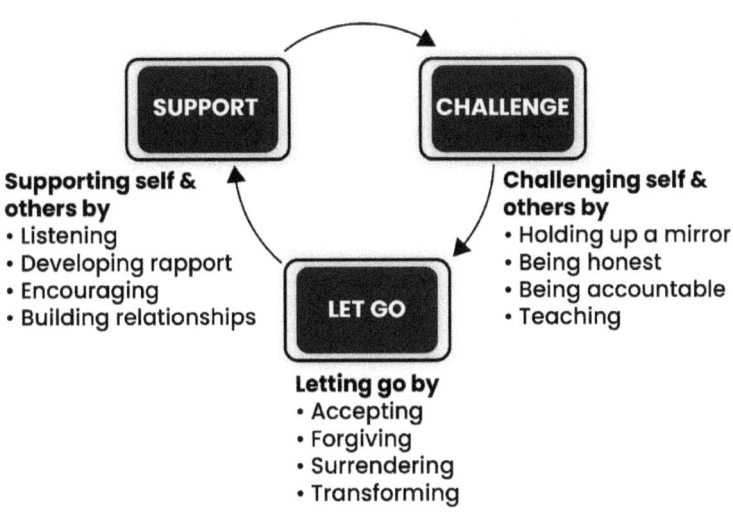

SUPPORT

CHALLENGE

LET GO

Supporting self & others by
• Listening
• Developing rapport
• Encouraging
• Building relationships

Challenging self & others by
• Holding up a mirror
• Being honest
• Being accountable
• Teaching

Letting go by
• Accepting
• Forgiving
• Surrendering
• Transforming

The first two elements of the Authentic Life Model are to support and challenge. These lead to a place where we can let go and experience an ongoing state of congruency and liberation. The support and challenge elements are action-based and provide opportunities to focus on ourselves, our personal relationships, and our organizations as leaders.

However, the letting go element of the model isn't as much about doing as it is about being. It's about releasing control and allowing things to flow. It's a beautiful dance between action and surrender that propels us toward living the *all is well*. That's where true freedom exists.

Sometimes, we can pour all our support, love, and comfort into others, yet deep down, there's a sense that something's missing in ourselves. Likewise, we may be fully engaged in challenging situations—learning, teaching, growing—and still feel like there's a void. It's this curious paradox that reminds us that true fulfillment often lies in the balance between supporting, challenging and letting go.

In my experience, some of us are geared to doing one more easily than the others, and that's okay. We're all unique and have different strengths, personalities, and experiences. The challenge is recognizing which we do well, continuing to do that, and working on the others.

Support

I'm always amazed when I see a story online or in the media in which someone steps up to lend a hand. These helpers are hailed as selfless heroes, answering the call of someone in need. Still, why does it catch us by surprise? Why is it newsworthy? Shouldn't acts of kindness be the norm among us? I wonder if these stories stand out because they're becoming less common.

Is it because showing love and compassion is seen as a sign of weakness compared to the more rigid approaches of challenging and instructing? Think about it. What we count is what we get. Our society values success, often measured by victories and accomplishments. Whether in sports, business, or the number of likes an influencer has, we cheer for triumph. However, isn't supporting and uplifting each other just as crucial?

Consider the support element of the Authentic Life Model both for ourselves and others. Self-support means listening to our inner voice, embracing who we are, and acknowledging our own worth. When it comes to supporting others, it's about listening, building rapport, showing respect, and offering healing.

It's vital to start with self-support. This demands self-awareness and conscious choices that add love and healing to our own lives. Yet, for many of us, accepting, loving, and healing ourselves is daunting. Until we truly embrace self-love and healing, how can we authentically support and care for others? When considering the golden rule of treating others as we would like to be treated, can we take that further? Think about how you speak to yourself. Are you as kind to yourself as you are to others? I sometimes find myself offering a kind word to someone that I wouldn't give to myself. How can this be right? If I reflect on how I talk about myself, am I frequently apologizing for who I am? Do I use negative language when describing myself? If so, I can change that.

We're not locked into or stuck with who we are; we're evolving every day. Amid life's chaos, love, support, and self-care can lead to profound personal growth and happiness and positively affect our mental health and the lives of those around us.

I am reminded of the story of the *Velveteen Rabbit*, a story that resonates with many. I loved this book as a child and read it to my children. Every Christmas, we would listen to Meryl Streep's version with the George Winston soundtrack—absolute gold! Just like the velveteen rabbit becomes "real" through love, we become our true selves through love and healing. Recognizing our worthiness allows us to receive and give love freely. What a great metaphor for our own lives. Just like the velveteen rabbit, love and healing make us real. They make us worthy of receiving love and healing and strengthen our ability to show it to others. If we are worthy, then we cannot be unworthy, no matter what.

We can all embrace the idea that we are worthy of love and healing, although for many, including myself, it can be challenging. When I screw up, hurt someone, or let someone down, I feel like crap. I feel less than or unworthy. The challenge is recognizing that worthiness is guaranteed. One thing I do when I'm feeling low is to remind myself that "All the forces of the universe conspired to create me… therefore, I am worthy!" You can repeat it like a sacred mantra every morning for a month while brushing your teeth and watch how it transforms your self-perception.

The journey to self-acceptance is challenging, especially with societal pressures and personal struggles. For many of us, this is a lifelong struggle. Our personalities, ambitions, goals, ego, environment, and the chaos in our lives all work against this concept of being worthy of love. Our media tend to feed us fear and chaos rather than supporting us in feeling worthy. However, supporting ourselves means striving to believe we are worthy of love and healing, no matter what life throws our way.

One of the best ways to kickstart your journey toward self-love and healing is through gratitude. Take a moment to appreciate yourself, your friends, your loved ones, and the incredible world we live in.

As we begin to tune into our own needs, we start the process of healing and cultivating self-love, and this can unlock a reservoir of power within ourselves. Suddenly, we become agents of positive change and love in the world. It's about listening intently, empathizing deeply, and demonstrating genuine care and love toward others.

So, how do we support others? What if you don't agree with someone or they have different beliefs or ideas than you? At its core, supporting others is about developing rapport, listening, and encouraging. You don't have to agree with someone to support them.

Story: Supporting People Over Politics

My friend Josh is passionate about politics, and he supports one particular party and candidate. His daughter, in her early 20s, is also passionate about politics; however, she has a completely different view from him and supports a different party.

They've had many heated discussions, arguments, and disagreements over what may or may not happen in the future and who our leaders should be. They were challenging each other, holding up the mirror, being honest, and pointing out facts and information. However, when I last caught up with Josh, he told me that he and his daughter had stopped talking to each other because of their differing political views.

We talked, and he said his daughter accused him of not loving and supporting her. I've known Josh for over 35 years, and he is a good man. He loves his daughter and would do anything for her. However, he disagrees with her political views and is unwilling to change his beliefs. He told me, "I don't want to lose her, but I won't compromise on my principles." I've no doubt that she'd say the same thing.

I find it odd that this has become a major disagreement within families and with friends across the US. Anyway, I asked Josh how he was supporting his daughter, and we talked about active listening and how he could show support for her. I challenged him to think about putting their relationship first and reminded him that his political views shouldn't define their relationship. It was there long before they had a difference of opinion.

A few weeks later, I ran into Josh and asked him how things were going with his daughter. He said they'd had a long talk, and things were improving. He'd let her know that he loved her and supported her and would always have her back. He also told her that although he respected her choice, he wouldn't vote for her candidate.

Now, his daughter didn't suddenly hug him, start crying, and say, "I love you, dad." She has a lot invested in her view, and it will take her some time to separate their different opinions from their relationship. However, she did thank him for having the conversation, and they're now talking again.

Like Josh, we choose what's important to us. In the Authentic Life Model, it's good to note that support comes before challenge. Often, we move into challenging others before we have taken the time to listen, build rapport, and offer support, which can cause problems.

Here are a few ways to put supporting others into practice:

❖ BE A ROCK IN THE STORM: Amid life's chaos, be a steadfast presence for those who need it. Take the time to show you care. Sometimes, all someone needs is for you to sit with them through tough times without trying to fix everything.

❖ LISTEN WITH YOUR HEART AND SOUL: Truly listening is an art. Try to understand what is happening in their lives and let them know they're heard and understood. We used to call this practicing active listening. It's not just about being physically present; it's about being emotionally present too.

❖ HOLD THEM UP: In a world where criticism reigns supreme, be a beacon of affirmation. Instead of cutting others down, build them up. Whether it's family dynamics or friendships, let go of negativity and choose to affirm and support. As a father, I've learned that my role isn't always about sharing my knowledge and experience and challenging my kids. It's also about being their biggest cheerleader, letting them know I'm proud of them, and always having their back.

If we embrace the power of gratitude, self-love, and support, we can create a ripple effect that transforms lives.

Challenge

This element of the Authentic Life Model deals with holding up the mirror to ourselves and others. It holds the promise of growth, enlightenment, and empowerment and is a dynamic blend of confronting challenges head-on while embracing the opportunity to teach, learn, and evolve.

Our society often hails the conquerors, the ones who boldly confront obstacles and emerge victorious. We enjoy tales of personal triumphs, whether they're measured in wealth, possessions, influence, or acclaim. Pursuing success isn't inherently flawed, but when it lacks support and balance, the costs can outweigh the gains. This is because it often means a winning-at-all-costs mentality. I don't believe this is sustainable. There are always costs. Our job is to ensure that, as authentic individuals, we challenge and win without destroying others.

Challenging ourselves or others isn't about picking fights; it's about holding up the mirror to reflect behaviors, actions, or truths, even when facing them is uncomfortable. By doing this, we open the doors to learning, growth, and improvement—the very essence of education. So, what's the best way to go on this journey of self-discovery and empowering others? Countless resources are available, offering insights into personal development, teaching, and learning.

I've always been fascinated by how we learn, and plenty of ideas, theories, and models are out there, each with its own unique approach. The easiest way to learn is to keep it simple, using these four key components: motivation, goals, action, and review:

MOTIVATION

Ever found yourself struggling to take that first step? Yeah, we've all been there. Still, it often boils down to one thing—motivation. It's that inner drive pushing us to change something about ourselves or our circumstances. It's about confronting ourselves, holding up that mirror, and understanding our motivation or why we want to do something.

Story: The Dean's Vacation

After my second year of college, I took what I like to refer to as "the dean's vacation." Actually, I got a letter from the college dean saying that my academic performance was so bad that I was being expelled. If I chose, I could reapply in 12 months, and they would assess my case and determine whether or not to allow me back.

What a pain! It didn't surprise me as I knew how badly I was doing. My parents were supportive but said that if I was going to move back home, I needed a plan. I didn't like a lot of things about myself—I was 40lbs. overweight from all the pizza and beer I'd be consuming, and I'd been kicked out of school. So, I decided to challenge myself. *Time to get motivated.* I decided to get a job and save some money. I began working out, watching what I ate, and soon lost the excess weight. With the money I saved, I backpacked through Europe and went on an Outward Bound program. During those 12 months, I learned a lot about life, overcoming challenges, and motivating myself more than any class at college could have taught me. When I did go back to college at the end of that year, I worked hard, and my results showed it. While my motivation to be a better version of myself was based on external factors, it required my internal drive to see it through.

Goals

Setting goals gives us direction, purpose, and something to strive for—they are the cornerstone of any journey. Think of goals like the GPS for your aspirations.

I remember being in a workshop once, and the facilitator was talking about SMART goals—Specific, Measurable, Achievable, Relevant, and Timely. At first, I thought it was kind of funny—I think a lot of things are funny, usually when they are not supposed to be; however, over the years, I've found this anagram useful when setting goals. You don't need to use the SMART model; the key is to find a goal-setting method that works for you and keeps you on track.

For me, setting goals isn't just about jotting down a list and calling it a day. I like diving into action right away. That's why I like the Now, Where, How approach. It's a no-nonsense way to turn goals into actionable plans, whether in my personal life or with teams and companies.

My mother used the metaphor of going to Raleigh to illustrate this concept. She would start by asking me the question—more often than I would have liked. Here's a retelling of that often-had conversation:

"Stephen, what's the first thing you need to know before you go to Raleigh?"

"Where Raleigh is," I'd say.

"Wrong! The first thing you need to know is why you're going. If you don't know why you're going or what your motivation is, then it doesn't matter where Raleigh is."

"Uh-huh," I'd say.

"What's the next thing you need to know when going to Raleigh?" she would ask.

"Where Raleigh is?" I'd answer.

"Wrong! You need to know where you are! If you first don't know where you are, then it doesn't matter where Raleigh is.

"Uh-huh," I'd respond.

"So, once you know why you're going, and you know where you are, what's the next question you need to answer?" she would ask.

"How I'm getting there?" I'd reply.

"Wrong! Now, you need to know where Raleigh is. If you don't know where you're going, then it's no use trying to figure out how to get there!"

"Right," I'd respond.

She would then give her final lesson. "Now that you know why you're going, where you are, and where Raleigh is. You can now figure out how to get to Raleigh."

I'd then give a list like, "Ride my bike, drive, take a plane, bus, walk."

The wild thing about this is that even though I'd get tired of repeatedly hearing this set of questions, they have served me well. It's a great model to put into practice when setting goals and planning. This works equally well for self-development, for staff, or groups.

Action

There's nothing quite as satisfying as rolling up my sleeves and getting things done. After going through the Now, Where, How process to clarify my goals, it's time to kick things into gear—it's time to act.

One of my favorite tools in the action phase is the 80/20 rule, also known as the Pareto principle. Developed by the Italian economist Vilfredo Pareto, it highlights the power of focus. Pareto found that 80% of outcomes often stem from just 20% of efforts. Think about it—we wear 20% of our clothes 80% of the time, 80% of our profits come from 20% of our customers, or 80% of our hassles come from 20% of our customers! When setting goals, using the 80/20 tool can help you prioritize what truly matters.

Once you've prioritized your goals, it's time to chart your course of action. This involves outlining the Who, What, When, How: Who is going to lead? Who do I need advice and support from? What specific tasks need to be accomplished? When's the deadline? How will I make it happen? And what resources do I need to succeed?

Review

Once you've developed your action items to meet your goals, regular review and reflection are key to staying on track. I recommend initially revisiting the goals every three to four days, then weekly. Once you've completed a goal, check it off and move on to the next goal.

By delving into the challenge element of the Authentic Life Model, we unlock some amazing benefits. Holding up the mirror to ourselves and others isn't just about reflection; it's about transformation, improvement, and growth.

Let go

So, now we come to the heart of the matter! Letting go isn't just a concept; it's the essence of living authentically. It holds the key to unlocking a life of fulfillment and joy, yet embracing it isn't always easy. While initially daunting, letting go eventually becomes a beacon of ease as we navigate the delicate balance between supporting and challenging ourselves and others. I've found that once I'm in a place of letting go, chaos dissipates, and it has little impact or effect on my life.

Letting go occurs when we relinquish attachment, control, or emotional investment in something. This can be a person, situation, belief, expectation, or even past experiences and memories. When we let go, we consciously decide to stop holding onto something that may be causing us stress or pain or blocking us from growing and developing.

Story: Confucius And The Waterfall

One of my favorite examples of letting go comes from the book *The Tao of Pooh* by Benjamin Hoff. In it, Hoff explains the concept of Wu Wei—acting without force, struggle, or ego—by recounting a story of Confucius by Chung-Tse. It goes something like this:

One day, Confucius and his disciples came upon a majestic waterfall cascading into a deep and turbulent pool. The sheer force of the water created powerful whirlpools and eddies, making it a dangerous place for any swimmer.

As Confucius and his disciples watched in awe, they noticed an old man being tossed about in the tumultuous water. The disciples feared the man would drown, but to their amazement, he emerged from the water unscathed and calm.

They rushed to him. "You must be a ghost," they said. "How are you alive, for surely nothing could survive that?" The old man looked at them and said, "I learned a long time ago, when I was a little boy, I go down with the water, and I come up with the water. When the water pushes, I yield; when it pulls, I follow. I do not fight the current."

This story is a great illustration of letting go. Just as the man in the waterfall survived by surrendering to the water's flow, we, too, can find peace by letting go of our need to control and resist. This approach not only reduces stress and struggle but also allows us to live more authentically, in tune with our true nature and the world around us.

My journey into letting go took an unexpected turn at a Buddhist retreat I attended after my divorce. I entered with a bit of a cocky attitude. I'd studied Buddhism in college and knew the basic concepts, ideas, and teachings. However, I was in pain. I was grieving. Despite my initial skepticism, I found myself humbled by the teachings of the Tibetan monks. It was here that I confronted the weight of my attachments. My pain was not caused by my actions or those of my ex. It was caused by my attachment to my ideas around love, commitment, and the expectations that had burdened me throughout my divorce. Understanding this was powerful stuff. I was able to begin the process of letting go. I still grieved, which hurt, but my perspective and focus had shifted. I was able to forgive and chart a new course.

At its core, letting go is about releasing control, resistance, and attachments and allowing things to unfold naturally. It's about releasing or relinquishing our attachment, control, or emotional investment in something. It involves consciously deciding to stop holding onto something that may be causing us stress, pain, or hindering our personal growth.

I remember that during a counseling session, the counselor shared the concept of attachments with me. She asked me to imagine going through life with a big bag strung over my shoulder—kind of like Santa's bag of toys, except these weren't toys. The bag stretched far behind me. It was heavy and getting in the way of me living a good life. In the bag were the pain, trauma, grief, grievances, conflicts, and "shit" I had experienced in my life. They were real, they happened, and I was carrying them with me. I couldn't just drop the bag and let go of them; it would have been too confronting, and I would have felt too vulnerable. What I could do, though, was take each one out, examine it, talk about it, and see how my attachment to the item allowed it to remain in the bag.

The counselor and I worked together over several sessions, and I was able to let go of many of the things in my bag as I realized that it was my attachment that was causing the pain. I still carry this bag over my shoulder. When it becomes heavy, I sift through the bag, pull things out, look at them, and figure out why I'm attached to them. I ask myself if each item still serves me. If it doesn't, I toss it. Today, the bag I carry over my shoulder is light and manageable.

Letting go isn't a one-time event; it's a gradual unfolding—a journey marked by introspection, acceptance, and, yes, vulnerability. Like shedding layers, it requires us to sift through our baggage, examining each attachment with honesty and compassion. Through this process, we make room for growth, resilience, and, ultimately, freedom.

I have a friend who said the things she carries—negative messages, trauma, fear, insecurity, self-loathing—are like hooks attached to a big, heavy coat—weighing her down. She used to put the coat on whenever things became tough, or she felt particularly low. It would just take her down further, but somehow, it was almost comforting because it was familiar to her. It's interesting to watch her journey as she has begun, in her words, "to make a new coat." "This one," she said, "is light and flowing—I can dance in it!" The coat is bright with a patchwork of colors representing all that she is grateful for—the love for and from her children, partner, and friends and the positive things in her life. She's been able to discard the old coat. Now, when negative messages or feelings from the past come up, she says there's no room for them on her new coat, and she's able to let them go. This is an incredible illustration of letting go.

Here are some key aspects that encompass the concept of letting go:

EMOTIONAL DETACHMENT: Letting go involves detaching emotionally from outcomes, people, or situations beyond our control. It doesn't necessarily mean we ignore emotions but acknowledge them while allowing them to flow without being consumed by them.

ACCEPTANCE: Letting go often requires us to accept the reality of chaos. It means acknowledging that certain things are beyond our control and that putting our energy into them may only lead to unnecessary suffering.

FORGIVENESS: Letting go means we forgive ourselves or others for past actions or mistakes. Remember, we're human. We make mistakes, we hurt the ones we love, and others hurt us. Holding onto grudges or regrets can keep us trapped in negative emotions and prevent us from moving forward.

FREEDOM: Letting go brings a sense of liberation. It frees us from past constraints, unproductive thought patterns, and the burden of trying to control every aspect of our lives.

PRESENT-MOMENT AWARENESS: Letting go encourages us to live in the present moment. When we release worries about the past or future, we can fully engage in the here and now.

PERSONAL GROWTH: By releasing attachments that no longer serve us, we create space for personal growth and new opportunities.

REDUCED STRESS: When we cling to things we cannot change, it contributes to stress and anxiety. Letting go helps to alleviate this stress by focusing on what we can influence and accepting what we cannot.

Letting go doesn't have to be a solitary pursuit. It thrives in the soil of community, nurtured by the support of loved ones and the wisdom of mentors. It's a dance between supporting and challenging—a delicate interplay that enriches our lives and fosters deep connections.

One of the critical things about the Authentic Life Model is that both supporting and challenging are equally valuable—and they complement each other. If you find yourself doing one more than the other, it's an opportunity to move the needle and work on the other area. I find it easier to challenge than support. I suspect this is true for many of us because supporting others requires a higher level of vulnerability. It can be uncomfortable to sit with others without offering advice, ideas, strategies, etc. So, try to be aware of this and strive for a balance. Remember, if you challenge without supporting or support without challenging, you'll be less effective.

Letting go is a journey of self-discovery. It is an opportunity to shift our focus away from a situation or person and move to a different place. By doing this, letting go becomes a major strength.

Story: Living An Authentic Life

Whether you're a Christian or not, the story of Jesus is fascinating, transcending religious boundaries and speaking to the essence of living authentically. He's a great example of someone who embodied the Authentic Life Model. He was a healer and teacher and practiced the art of letting go like few before or since.

As a healer, Jesus performed miracles. He raised Lazarus from the dead and healed people who were crippled, blind, or had leprosy. Yet, his healing wasn't confined to physical ailments; it extended to the wounded souls of those he encountered. He listened, laughed, empathized, and connected on a level beyond the superficial. It's a reminder that true healing isn't just about fixing bodies but about nurturing spirits.

As a teacher, he practiced the art of discipline. He was one of the original stoics. He asked questions like a Socratic bard. Even as a boy, he was found sitting among the teachers in the temple, asking them questions. In fact, Jesus is recorded as asking 307 questions in the Gospels.

In contrast, he directly answers only three of the 183 questions he was asked. Jesus didn't just impart knowledge; he sparked introspection, challenging the status quo with every probing question. In a world obsessed with answers, he showed the power of questioning, of holding up the mirror to society's flaws.

Then, as his life came to an end, he pulled off the ultimate act of letting go—giving his life, his entire self, to completely let go. It's a great lesson in the art of release, a reminder that true freedom lies in relinquishing control.

Yet, amidst the miracles and teachings, it's Jesus' humanity that resonates most deeply with me. He wasn't some distant deity; he was a man who felt joy and pain. He partied, laughed, and hung out with people. He struggled and had doubts about himself and others. He felt anger, sadness, and betrayal, just like us. He lived and experienced real chaos.

We can seize on these ideas for our own lives. We can recognize our own worthiness and capacity for love and happiness. By doing so, we not only enrich our own lives, but we can also help others see their worthiness and guide them toward their own path of authenticity and fulfillment.

Opportunities authenticity provides for living our best lives

The impact of living an authentic life can be profound for ourselves and our relationships, including:

❖ IMPROVED MENTAL HEALTH: Living authentically means we can challenge and let go of negative emotions and experiences that can negatively impact our mental wellbeing. It allows us to focus on positivity and gratitude.

❖ ENHANCED RELATIONSHIPS: Living authentically means we have the opportunity to understand and be aware of our expectations and attachments in relationships, leading to healthier interactions. It enables us to appreciate people for who they are rather than trying to meld them into our expectations.

❖ PERSONAL DEVELOPMENT: Living authentically means we hold up the mirror to ourselves and develop new goals for self-improvement. It allows us to move the dial in our own lives from where we are to where we want to be.

❖ HEIGHTENED CURIOSITY: By living authentically, we become more curious and ask more questions. We can let go of rigid ideas and attachments and instead stimulate creativity and innovation. It opens up space for new ideas and perspectives to emerge.

❖ INNER PEACE: Living authentically often brings a sense of inner peace. It allows us to experience a greater sense of contentment and harmony within ourselves and the world around us.

Essentially, living authentically is about consciously choosing to live and wrestle with the paradox. It means we can live lives with less emotional baggage and more openness to the present moment. It's a process that requires self-awareness, practice, and a willingness to embrace change. While it may be challenging at times, the rewards for personal growth and overall wellbeing can be significant.

LIFE HACKS

Support
There are many ways you can support yourself.

JOURNALING
In your journal, fill a page with words that describe your strengths and gifts. Refer to them occasionally and add to them as you achieve goals and experience wins or victories.

ACTIONS
Listen to the way you talk to yourself. Remove yourself from harmful people and chaos if necessary. Another way to support yourself is to create a positive mantra that you repeat to yourself daily. I like to say, "I'm alive, therefore I'm worthy!"

Challenge
ACTIONS
Holding up the mirror to ourselves is important. Seek feedback from a friend or someone you trust. Ask them to give you feedback on how you handled a situation, what they think your strengths and weaknesses are, opportunities for improvement, etc. Think about the feedback, and if you want to change or improve, then create a plan and set some goals.

Let go
MINDFULNESS
Just like the old man in the waterfall story, think about how you can go up and down with the water and not fight or resist.

Here's something you can try. Think about the things in your life you're holding onto. Maybe it's a grudge against someone who hurt you. Perhaps it's the pain of loss or grief or a mindset that keeps you stuck in a rut. Ask yourself what the worst thing would be if you let it go. Then, ask yourself what's the best thing that could happen by letting it go.

ACTIONS

Once you have reflected on the things you want to let go of, write them down on a piece of paper. Next, light a "ritual" fire—either in the fireplace or an outdoor campfire. Toss the piece of paper into the fire and say to yourself, "I'm letting you go." I've done this with friends, and it's a great way to exorcise some of those personal demons.

17

LOVE

AS THE SAYING GOES, "All you need is love." I'm not talking about some new-age philosophy of loving the world and coming to-gether, holding hands, and singing—although that would be some-thing to witness. If we choose love as the cornerstone of our actions and intentions, it can help us hold the line amidst the chaos.

Love is an amazing thing we get to experience as humans. It's the ultimate expression of living the *all is well*. Love is the emotional foundation that inspires and fuels genuine, selfless acts of care and concern. Love—whether for ourselves or others—inspires qualities like:

❖ Kindness;

❖ Empathy;

❖ Compassion;

❖ Generosity;

❖ Patience;

❖ Gratitude;

- ❖ Trust;

- ❖ Courage;

- ❖ Joy;

- ❖ Forgiveness.

Love often begets love, creating a positive feedback loop that can enhance personal and collective resilience. Showing love brings joy, both to the giver and the receiver. However, it doesn't always yield the response we anticipate or desire. Sometimes, loving others can be met with indifference or even hostility. It's at times like these that we need to double down on love. We show love in the ways listed above because it's right. If it makes us feel good, then that's a bonus. If it doesn't, it's still right. I challenge you to think of one person you can show love to today. It doesn't have to be a grand gesture; even the smallest act of gratitude or kindness can make a world of difference to someone in need.

Love in the form of kindness demands little from us but can positively impact those around us. In our chaotic world of digital interactions and face-to-face transactions, genuine acts of kindness can feel like a breath of fresh air. It's about making an authentic connection, leaving a positive impact that lingers long after the interaction ends. As a bonus, demonstrating kindness is good for us, improving mental and physical health, reducing stress, and promoting happiness and a sense of fulfillment.

Love multiplies, hate divides

Love is the only truly sustainable human characteristic, condition, and emotion. Love acts as a multiplier—it can build on itself and keep growing. When present, love enhances positive emotions like kindness, gratitude, and compassion, which strengthen relationships. The effects of love can spread, creating a ripple effect that benefits not only us individually but also those around us.

Hate, on the other hand, functions as a divider. It breaks down relationships, creates rifts, and builds division. When present, hate generates negative emotions such as anger, resentment, and hostility. These emotions can make us feel isolated, eroding trust and disrupting social cohesion. Hate divides communities by creating an us-versus-them mentality, leading to conflicts and perpetuating cycles of animosity. Hate ultimately consumes itself.

Throughout history, every empire, government, political movement, religion, teaching, and philosophy rooted in hate has been defeated from the outside or eventually killed itself off.

Story: Love And Kindness

Michelle and Denis are two of my closest friends. We met while working at a summer camp in Western North Carolina over a few summers, then separately moved to Australia some years later. They lived close by in Australia, and our children grew up together.

I consider Denis my best mate and Michelle my best friend. "Mate" is a quintessential Australian term that implies a sense of shared experience, mutual respect, loyalty, and unconditional assistance. It crosses racial and gender lines, and it's also a term of endearment. I remember sharing with Michelle and Denis how I viewed them one day, and Michelle asked, "Why can't I be your mate and Denis be your friend?" I replied, "Well, Michelle, if you have to ask, then you don't know, and the question answers itself."

My relationship with Denis is based more on our shared experience as middle-aged men trying to raise our kids, be good husbands, and be good friends, offering kindness in a wild, chaotic world. There's an unspoken trust. We'll sometimes have deep and meaningful conversations, but mostly, we chill, have a beer, and talk about nothing in particular. We feel and think deeply about things, but we don't always talk about them.

Aside from my wife, Michelle is my closest friend. We've had many deep and meaningful conversations about life, relationships, politics, religion, children, values, and much more over the years. Michelle, like any good friend, can listen well and support you but also challenges you to be better.

So, when my marriage broke up, and it became hectic and chaotic, I called Michelle. For about three or four weeks, at the height of the madness, I rang her daily. I vented, ranted, cried, and shared with her. She listened. She didn't judge me or critique my comments or decisions. She offered words of support and encouragement and let me know I wasn't alone, that I had friends and family who loved me, and that I would be okay. She showed me kindness by being there and allowing me the space to process the pain I was feeling.

Michelle would also stand up for me when I wasn't around. I heard from an acquaintance that some parents were waiting for their children after school one day, gossiping and having a go at me. I was not there to defend myself. However, Michelle overheard the conversation and challenged them. She told them I was a good man and a good father and that they obviously didn't have all the facts. The wild thing is that being my friend and supporting me cost her personally. She lost at least one friendship that I know of.

Every couple of weeks during that time, Denis would call and ask if I wanted to go have a beer. We would sit and talk and just be. Yep, he's my mate.

I'll always be grateful to Denis and Michelle for the love, support, kindness, and friendship they showed me when I was in chaos. They each expressed their love differently, and I relied on them for different things, but they showed up and stood with me. Our strong bond continues to this day.

Opportunities love provides for living our best lives

Love acts as the shield and sword for living in the *all is well*. It can counteract chaos and defeat negative emotions and behaviors like hate, toxicity, and anger. Here are some examples:

- ❖ BUILDING POSITIVE RELATIONSHIPS: Love fosters strong, supportive relationships, which can provide a buffer against negative emotions.

- ❖ CREATING A POSITIVE ENVIRONMENT: Acts of kindness can create an atmosphere where negative behaviors are less likely to thrive.

- ❖ MODELING POSITIVE BEHAVIOR: Demonstrating love can inspire others to act similarly, creating a ripple effect.

- ❖ ENCOURAGING FORGIVENESS AND RECONCILIATION: Love can pave the way for forgiveness and reconciliation, breaking cycles of resentment and retaliation.

- ❖ PROMOTING MENTAL AND EMOTIONAL WELLBEING: Expressions of love contribute to better mental health, reducing the likelihood of negative emotions taking root.

❖ DEFUSING TENSION AND CONFLICT: Responding to anger and hostility with calmness and understanding can deescalate situations and prevent the spread of negativity.

LIFE HACKS

JOURNALING
Spend some time thinking and journaling about love. As you do, start with yourself and then others. Here are some questions to get you started:

❖ What are five things I love about myself?

❖ When was the last time I did something for myself, and how did that make me feel?

❖ What are three accomplishments I'm proud of?

❖ Who uplifts me each time I'm with them?

❖ What are three acts of kindness I've done for others recently? How did it make me feel to do those things?

❖ Who is one person I can show love or an act of kindness to in the next 24 hours? What will I do?

ACTIONS
12 in 24 Challenge: Give yourself the challenge to demonstrate 12 acts of kindness to others in the next 24 hours. Maybe you buy someone a cup of coffee, leave someone a note, give someone a hug or words of encouragement, pay it forward at the drive-thru, or have a conversation with a stranger. The opportunities are endless. When you're done, you may want to reflect on the experience in your journal.

18

BRINGING IT ALL TOGETHER

LIFE IS CHAOS! IT SURROUNDS us, penetrates us, and sometimes it feels like it's consuming us. Amid the turmoil, we can find ourselves grappling with trauma, anxiety, and fear. Yet, within this chaos lies a beacon of hope—the opportunity to live a life full of joy. A life in which we're aware of our actions and choices and choose to live authentically with gratitude. We can be overwhelmed by the chaos or focus on living in the *all is well.* By tapping into the resilience in all of us, we can move more freely between chaos and calm.

In my youth, I spent many long summer nights in the mountains of Western North Carolina. Whether at summer camp, some weekend retreat my family was attending, or a folk dancing workshop at school, I seemed to do a lot of square dancing. We tended to refer to it as mountain circle dancing, but there was also clogging or flatfoot dancing. I enjoyed those dances. They had a pattern and sense of order. If you followed the caller's instructions, 50 to 100 people could move in unison to the music. However, some would inevitably spin the wrong way, move in the wrong direction, or mix up the difference between swinging their corner or partner. Amid the order of the dance, there was chaos.

I see our lives as dances. Whether it's square dancing, ballet, hip hop, ballroom, or freestyling in a mosh pit, for most of us, dancing can fill us with joy. When something unexpected happens—we take a wrong step or get spun in the wrong direction—it's best to go with the spin and move back into the rhythm and flow of the dance. This is how I see moving between chaos and the *all is well*. If we can allow ourselves to go with the flow rather than fight against the chaos, we can find joy. Everyone dances differently, but with practice, discipline, and focus, we can learn to move smoothly and lightly between these two states of living without letting the chaos derail or ruin us.

Story: Special Steve

As a child, I always looked forward to the new school year but also had a lot of anxiety about it. I generally enjoyed school but disliked the standardized tests. I've never been one to excel in such settings. While logically, I understood that these tests weren't about passing or failing but rather about assessing where I stood compared to my peers, emotionally, I felt like a failure.

So, you can imagine my surprise when, after taking one of these tests at the end of my 6th-grade year, I was promptly directed to a different classroom at the beginning of my 7th-grade year.

Stepping into that new classroom, I was met with a startling revelation: I had been placed in what was colloquially referred to as the "special class." It was a diverse mix of individuals—students with learning disabilities, severe intellectual disabilities, those diagnosed with autism, and even newcomers from Vietnam and Laos who were just beginning to speak English. "What the hell is going on!" I muttered to myself, caught in a whirlpool of chaos ranging from anger to embarrassment to sheer terror. I felt lost in the chaos, unsure of my place.

Returning home that day, I poured out my frustrations to my parents, seeking solace and guidance. Two days later, they met with the principal; however, the resolution was far from immediate. I would have to remain in this unfamiliar environment for a couple of months until my grades improved. I was granted a partial reprieve—I could attend my old homeroom, have lunch with my friends, and participate in a few elective classes like drama. Yet, for the bulk of my day, I was confined to the "special class."

Except for my brothers calling me Special Steve, a name they still use to this day, my family were pretty supportive. My parents decided to make this experience a learning opportunity. They sat me down and told me that this was the way it was—I could get angry, or I could get on with it. They held up the mirror to me and challenged me to make it work for me—not make the best of it, but make it work for me. So, I did. I stopped ignoring the kids in the "special class" and made friends with them. They accepted me and were incredible. They were all different, but I soon learned that they each had gifts and strengths, and I began to admire their uniqueness.

We learned and laughed together, and when I did eventually return to the mainstream class, I continued my friendship with many of them. I'd invite them to sit with me and my friends at lunch and often play with them at recess. I convinced some of my friends to help, and we ended up tutoring many of the kids after school. With the help of my parents, teachers, and new friends, I made it work for me. I stopped focusing on the chaos and began to live into the *all is well*. My awareness increased, and I learned new things and let go of many of the perceptions I'd had about these kids and even myself. What started as a traumatic year ended up being one of my best school years.

In this story lies the essence of life's chaos—unexpected twists, unwelcome surprises, and the resilience required to navigate it all. However, amid the turbulence, there's also an opportunity to experience the *all is well*. Even in the face of adversity, our choices, actions, and outlook shape our journey, determining whether we succumb to the chaos or rise above it.

I often reflect on that 7th-grade year. In many ways, I found it easier to navigate the chaos then. Maybe with age, I'm less courageous. Perhaps I want to avoid pain and hurt whenever I can rather than make it work for me. Whatever the reason, I try to remind myself that I still have the strength of my 7th-grade self and much more. I'm more battle-scarred and wiser, and I work at being more compassionate and less judgmental. I try to approach each new day with gratitude and hope.

Living our best lives requires us to redirect our focus toward the things that enrich our lives, acknowledging that while challenges like fear, anxiety, trauma, and grief may persist, they don't define us. If we channel our focus and energy into self-awareness, intentional choices, gratitude, resilience, and living with authenticity, we better equip ourselves to confront life's adversities. By doing so, a remarkable shift occurs: the chaos diminishes as the joy of living intensifies.

Where to from here?

I'm often asked, "How do I live in the *all is well?*" Foremost, remember that it's a journey. It has taken me many years and false starts to develop the practices and routines that support me in living my best life. Some days, I feel like things are really rockin', and I have it together. Other days, chaos seems to take over, and I feel like crap. Still, that's okay; it's normal. Remember, the chaos is always there. However, through daily practices, rituals, intent, and discipline, we can live our best lives every day. Here are some things you may want to try on your journey into the *all is well*:

❖ LEARN: There are so many amazing resources out there, including books, podcasts, social media, and speakers to help you gain knowledge, develop skills, and try new things. I have mentioned a few in this book. Spend time each week exploring concepts such as awareness, gratitude, choices, authenticity, resilience, and love. Set a goal to learn something new every day. Knowledge is power!

❖ BE MINDFUL: Develop daily routines and practices around mindfulness and meditation. It's funny; I used to resist the whole meditation thing as I thought it was a bit hokey, but now it's a critical part of my daily routine. I've found that it allows me to engage in chaos like fear and anxiety without having to lose myself. I can recognize the thoughts and feelings of being anxious or afraid, accept them, and move on. By doing this, they have little or no power over me.

❖ ACT: Less talk, more action. Showing others love, kindness, gratitude, and forgiveness is the right action. Being intentional in how we treat ourselves and others daily is the best defense against chaos.

If true joy is indeed found in the pursuit of living our best lives, then it's a pursuit worthy of our attention and effort. Living an *all-is-well* life is a balancing act. When things are going well within myself, my relationships, and at work, I tend to attract the positive. However, I simultaneously seem to attract chaos. This may sound like a contradiction, but this is similar to magnets. Each has a north and a south pole, and when you place the north pole of one magnet near the south pole of another magnet, they are attracted to one another. Conversely, the north poles of magnets repel each other.

Therefore, when we're in chaos, we seem to attract more chaos, and when we're living well, we tend to attract the good. However, there's also the opposite effect. So, when we are living our best lives and things are going well, we need to be open to more abundance and good things, but at the same time, keep an eye out for chaos. It may be under the surface or around the corner, but it's always there. You cannot separate an *all-is-well* life from chaos. I hope you find the balance to endure the chaos while enjoying your best life.

ACKNOWLEDGMENTS

Thank you to my brothers, David and Daniel. Your insights, humor, and support are immeasurable.

Thank you to my mother and father. Mom, your insights are invaluable. Dad, you are missed.

To my many friends and colleagues who have helped shape my journey and given me the strength and courage to live through the chaos and into the *all is well*.

HEY THERE
AWESOME READER

YOU'VE MADE IT TO THE END – CONGRATS!

If you found any nuggets of wisdom, humor, or at least a few moments of "Aha!", I'd be thrilled if you could leave a review on Amazon. Think of it as your good deed for the day. With your help, we can keep the motivation rolling and maybe even save the world from a zombie apocalypse. Thanks.

P.S. – Need a business consultant or a speaker for your next conference? Yep, that's me! Book now and get a free zombie survival tip with every gig. Go to <u>winningchaos.com</u>

www.ingramcontent.com/pod-product-compliance
Lightning Source LLC
Chambersburg PA
CBHW051313120626
46547CB00015B/2218